Country Preacher's Notebook

Book II

Stories and

meditations

reflecting

the spirit

of rural

people

by Joyce Sasse

Cover and inside cover photo: Joyce Sasse's picture of volunteers re-siding a village church pays tribute to the endless hours of "sweat equity" given to build and maintain facilities and keep life going in rural communities.

Country Preacher's Notebook, Book II

DESIGNED & PRODUCED BY
breaking ground communications
BOX 98, PINCHER CREEK, AB T0K 1W0

Canadian Cataloguing in Publication Data

Sasse, Joyce.
    Country Preacher's Notebook, Book Two

    ISBN 0-9682920-0-3

Published by
Country Preacher Publications
Box 92, Pincher Creek, AB, Canada T0K 1W0

Printed in Canada by
Quality Color Press Inc.,
18330 - 102 Avenue
Edmonton, AB, T5S 2J9

Permissions

Chicken Soup written by Nicholas Klempa of Calgary, AB. Used by Permission of the author.

Paraphrases of Psalms 8, 23, 32, 118, 121 from <u>Everyday Psalms</u> by James Taylor, published by Wood Lake Books, Inc. Copyright (c) 1994 Wood Lake Books, Inc. Used with permission.

Ford Closed Car advertisement used with permission of the Ford Motor Company of Canada, Limited.

Quotation of Carl Dudley. from *Making The Small Church Effective*, used with permission of Abingdon Press/Cokesbury.

My Father Johnny Green written by Jim Green of Fort Smith, N.W.T. Used by permission of the author.

Dance Little Jean, written by Jim Ibbotson (c) 1988 UNAMI Music (ASCAP) / Administered by BUG MUSIC. All Rights Reserved. Used by permission.

The Servant Song by Richard Gillard. (c) 1977 Scripture In Song (a div. of Integrity Music, Inc). All rights reserved, International copyright secured. Used by Permission. c/o Integrity Music, Inc. P.O. Box 851622, Mobile, AL 36685.

Excerpts from *Facing The Tiger* by Shirley Endicot. Used by permission of the author.

Julia - A Memoir written by Diane Burt Stuckey of Pincher Creek, Alta. Used by permission of the author.

Grandfather's Open Arms written by Erin Phillips of Lethbridge, Alberta. Reprinted from the Lethbridge Herald, July 12, 1997. Used by permission of the author.

Tribute to Darryl Vance written by Linda Austen of Hill spring, Alta. Used by permission of the author.

Rick Hansen *"Man in Motion"* Commemorative Plate used with permission from Waterford Wedgwood Canada Inc.

Give To Us Laughter, written by Walter Farquharson. Used by permission of the author.

Contents

Expressions Of Faith   89

Introduction

A Country Preacher has opportunity to participate in rural community life in a particular way. I treasure that opportunity. It has given me a chance to enter into the very centre of people's lives: to cry with them in their pain, to help celebrate their joy, and to enjoy the wry humour. Along the way, I try to help them name those spiritual sources from whence they find strength and courage.

As a farm girl raised in southern Alberta, I have never really gotten the soil out from under my fingernails. It is a part of me. As a country preacher who has worked through years of drought and decades of social change, I have tried to live prayerfully in the midst of often grieving communities. As a theologian by instinct and training, my life has been enriched as I witnessed the devout tenacity of so many.

A lot of these people are not regular church attenders. Only a few feel comfortable participating in a study group. Several have dropped out of the organized life of the institutional church ... But that doesn't mean they are spiritually bereft. They know they have often been touched by God's grace. And they are genuinely appreciative when someone can make linkages between their life-experience, the Gospel Story, and the Church.

The three sections of my manuscript are: Being Rural, Experiencing The Pain, and Expressions of Faith. My concern is to help record some of the stories, share some of the reflections, and pass on bits of the humour found in rural living. At the same time, I sincerely hope nothing here will betray entrusted confidentialities.

I want to express my gratitude to the various individuals whose writings are included. Jim Taylor, Ralph Milton, Diane Burt-Stuckey, and the others are wonderful mentors and friends.

This is not a book that should be read in one sitting. Select one story here. Let another speak from over there. In-between, pause to reflect on your own story ... or recall someone who's life has touched yours. Then set the book aside fOR a while. Go for a walk in the garden of life, and let the arms of a loving God enfold you.

Joyce Sasse

"This book is dedicated to the gifted ministry of faith filled friends."

Being Rural

Mt. Mill Church

    Put-downs and criticisms directed at those who live in small communities often come from people who do not understand the importance of being rooted in the land. They have not walked across the earth in bare feet; they have not felt its heartbeat. They have not been stirred by the mystery of life bursting forth under a warm spring rain. They have not been quieted by the beauty of a sunset. They have not cried out because they felt the pain of the land suffering from drought.

    Outsiders may laugh at the homely ways of rural folk and point to quaint customs. But they do not understand how a community can become like an extended family, whose members have a vested interest in each other. Drawn shades, a snowy sidewalk not swept by noon, a light in the wee small hours - each of these tells its own story of illness, or upset, or tragedy to neighbors keeping a caring watch.

    I'm proud to say that I live in a small community. By choice. That's where I want to be. That's where I need to be... I hope the items on the following pages help to show why.

When Things Go Bang in The Night

*Whether prairie folk meet each other as they pick up groceries in
the Moose Jaw Coop, or as they stroll the streets of downtown
Honolulu, they start their conversation with comments and queries
about the weather. This is Big Sky Country. What happens in those
skies constantly impacts our lives.*

Around Pincher Creek, Alberta, you can awake to
find the Chinook wind has rolled fields full of twenty
inch snow balls.

Around Eyebrow, Saskatchewan, you look out first
thing to see a twister has taken the roof off the cattle
shed and smashed your steel granary.

Near Empress, Alberta, huge thunderheads build and
turn ugly.
Then, about the time you want to go to bed, they
release a bone-jarring cosmic light and sound show.

On Highway # 11, near Davidson, Saskatchewan, the
yellow and white lines on the highway
become completely obliterated by fog as you grope
your way home on a November evening.

On Highway # 2, out of Claresholm, Alberta, the
night is filled with terror
as you feel for the edge of the road when caught in a
sudden blinding blizzard.

Major power poles are snapped by the weight of
snow from a late May storm.

Thousands of brooder chicks become chilled and die.

A woman turns onto a side road two miles before she should have, and gets stuck fast.
She sits there for 24 hours in minus thirty degree weather until conditions clear enough for a 'chopper' to take off and spot her.

A farmer wakens to find that the grain on each of his ten quarter sections of crop has been laid flat by last night's hail.
The nauseating stench of pulverized, fermenting growth turns his stomach.

Tears of pain roll down a young woman's face as she tries to nurse a horse whose body has been bruised by baseball-sized hailstones.
The eye is gone ... The terror of the night is evident in the way the horse shivers and flinches through the next day ... and the days after that!

An endless litany of true stories ... life threatening stories involving our person, our crops, our livestock, our livelihood.

We have heard the weather man, from his air-conditioned studio, complain that there might be rain on the weekend, while our crops are burning up because of extended drought.

We have heard the insurance adjusters compare the luck of the farmers, during a recent spring flood, with the suffering of the town folk who got hit. They do this because their forms have no space to list the washed away fence lines, the twisted corrals, the tons of top soil vanished, and the fields where grass will have to be re-seeded.

We have heard the snickers and comments about farmers "always needing something to complain about." The words are said thoughtlessly by those who have never had half their yearly income wiped out by a single storm. The words are said thoughtlessly by those who wear snow boots only when they are headed off to the ski slopes. The words are said thoughtlessly by summer farm visitors who relish a meal of garden fresh peas and potatoes, but have never hoed and watered a plot of their own. A June frost means nothing to them.

One could continue the litany of weather woes. But for country folk this litany is no dirge. in spite of the extremes of winter and the momentous blows that strike us down in the summer ... In spite of the scourge that brings with it the grasshoppers and army worms and gophers ... In spite of the fact that our lives and livelihoods seem so meager as compared with the powers of nature ... We not only carry on, but we understand ourselves to be co-partners with God in creation. We do what we can, trusting ourselves into the hands of a Greater Power. Time and again we stand together with the psalmists and poets of old, who also lived close to the land, who faced the adversities of the skies, and who could still celebrate "the glorious power of God."

Psalm 29   The Lord of the Seven Thunders

In a violent storm, reverberating peals of thunder suggest to the psalmist the commanding "voice of the Lord." Thus are the people summoned to worship the mighty King, who blesses this people with peace and well-being.

Give unto the Lord, O heavenly beings,
give unto the Lord glory and strength!
Give unto the Lord the glory due unto his name;
worship the Lord in holy array!

The voice of the Lord is upon the waters;
the God of glory thunders.
The voice of the Lord is powerful,
the Lord is full of majesty.

The voice of the Lord breaks the cedars,
the Lord breaks the cedars of Lebanon.
The voice of the Lord make Lebanon skip like a calf,
and Sirion like a young wild ox.

The voice of the Lord flashes forth flames of fire,
the voice of the Lord shakes the wilderness,
the Lord shakes the wilderness of Kadesh.
The voice of the Lord makes the oaks to whirl
and strips the forests bare;
and in his temple everything cries, "Glory!"

The Lord sits enthroned over the flood;
the Lord sits enthroned as King for ever.
May the Lord give strength to his people!
May the Lord bless his people with peace!

Chicken Soup
written by Nick Klempa

Nick's Grandmother was also my special friend. She welcomed all of us with bowls of homemade chicken noodle soup. Nick was nine years old when she died. Eight years later he still remembered, and wrote the following for a high school assignment.

My grandmother died when I was still very young, so I don't have many memories of her. I do, however, remember all those visits we made to the farm where she lived. The three hour ride, the fights I had with my sisters, the country music station my father listened to, and the sigh of relief we all let out when we saw just a glimpse of the farm in the distance - all are very strong memories. And the food. We could smell the food as soon as we stepped out of the car, a blend of every one's favorites cooking on the stove. Grandma would deny that she had been cooking all day and that she had it prepared days before she even knew we were coming.

Mom knew better and knew that Grandma had been up early that morning to make my favorite meal, chicken soup. She would first kill the chicken and clean it before going to the immaculately kept garden and pulling the fresh carrots and parsley. Then leaving that to cook, she would start making the noodles, cutting each one by hand. I always thought that if she could have somehow had time to grind the flour she would have done that too; maybe she did. That soup always tasted so good. In a restaurant Grandma could have charged five dollars a bowl easily. But all I had to do was smile and give her a hug after dinner.

Staring down at my hamburger and fries, I wondered if the dolt, with the paper hat, behind the counter made them with as much love as Grandma made my soup. Not that I would go give that fat greasy thing a hug after I was finished, even if he did. My grandmother would be ashamed of me if she was alive, to see me in a place like this. Eating with my hands out of paper boxes with speeds faster than that at which the food was made. Sorry, Grandma but that's how the world is operating now!

People do not have or make the time to do anything for themselves. You would probably think it funny if you were here but you can go to almost any fast food outlet and for no extra charge you can have them hurtle your food into your car as you drive by. This is the foremost in impersonal service, but I'm sure that they will find yet another way to make it worse. However, if given the option of going inside and talking to the employees face to face or yelling into a wooden sign, I'll take the wooden sign. It looks and smells a lot better.

However, if you opt to go inside, reader beware. The employees find it necessary to ask you if you would like fries with that, no matter what you order. The eating atmosphere is nothing like you would find at Grandma's, a tacky display of the company's colors and self-promoting slogans plastered across the greasy walls. People run in and out, not bothering to clean up after themselves.

I sat at home recently and watched people line up for hours in Moscow to experience the same thing. Is this the way people are going to eat in the future? I wondered if my children would ever get a chance to taste Grandma's chicken soup.

Awe and Wonder

Paraphrase of Psalm 8

Jim Taylor's paraphrases are not meant to replace the Psalms as we find them in Scripture. But the fresh wording helps me think about these ancient truths in the context of my own life experience.

My God, my God
how wonderful you are!
There is nothing like you in the whole earth.

I look up to the skies, and I see you there;
Babies and infants open their mouths,
and I hear them cry your name.
Compared to you, our weapons, our bombs,
our power to destroy,
dwindle into insignificance.
On a starry night, with your glory splashed across the
skies,
I gaze into your infinite universe, and I wonder:
Who am I?
Why do I matter?
Why do you care about mere mortals?

We humans are less than specks of dust in your universe.
We have existed less than a second in the great clock of
creation.
Yet you choose us as your partners.
You share the secrets of the universe with us;
you give us a special place in your household;
you trust us to look after the earth, on your behalf -
not just the sheep and oxen,
but also the wolves that prey on our domestic animals;
the birds, the plants, and even creatures we have never seen

in the depth of the sea.
My God, my God! How amazing you are!

by James Taylor

Meditation On A Clump Of Prairie Sod

*"I find letters from God dropped in the street
and every one is signed by God's name."*
Walt Whitman

*We find wonderful messages in surprising places. All we need are
the eyes to see.*

Land is more than a place on which we build our
houses, and plough our fields, and pasture our cattle.
Land is a gift - a gift from God. God said to the people
of Israel, as they were about to cross the Jordan into
Israel

*"The land that you are about to enter is a land of moun-
tains and valleys, a land watered by rain. The Lord your
God takes care of the land and watches over it throughout the year." (Deuteronomy 11: 11, 12)*

Land is a gift .. and God can speak to us through this
gift.

I grew up in the midst of short-grass country ... Our
family spent many a spring day fighting to try to stop the
constant soil drifting that cut through our fields, one after
another. You see, our land should never have been
ploughed. The natural prairie sod should never have
been broken.

Just a few miles away, in the Milk River Ridge, the managers of the McIntyre Ranch teach us the values inherent in maintaining good prairie sod.

The real story lies in the underground network of tough fiber root in natural sod. It is dense, like a buffalo robe. If you look closely, you will see that prairie sod is made up of an intricate system of many species of plants living in close relationship. There you find grass, shrubs, and broad leaf plants ... Some to trap the water, some to break the wind, some to cover the dry soil during a drought ... The strategy for success lies in each plant living in harmony with a wide variety of neighbors. Furthermore, even after separate plants have died, or gone dormant, the mat of compost-like material protects and gives nutrients back to the soil. This intricate network of life enables prairie sod to withstand the bitter cold, the burning heat, the prairie fires, and the parching wind.

There is a sermon in the story of the sod ... a sermon that instructs us how to live as a People of God.

First, we need to recognize that we are gifted!

Too many pioneers were deaf to the message the land told, because they insisted their ways were better. "Break the sod," they said. "Cultivate it! Make the land produce!" But the verities of the land nearly defeated these entrepreneurs during the Thirties ... There was a very real threat that the land would become desert, and the desert would consume hundred of thousands of acres. (See the story of this struggle in the book Men Against The Desert by James Gray.)

God has gifted us in the same way ... We have been

created as unique and special persons ... with the potential to live rich, fulfilling lives .. But if we fail to listen ... if we ignore the need for prayerful reflection ... the rigours of life might more easily consume our being?

Second, meditating on a clump of sod could help us be more appreciative of the importance of living in community.

Diversity of growth is the important thing in giving fiber and toughness to the prairie sod. Should we be more mindful of this strategy for success in our own community? Are we not stronger because of our diversity? As we reach across age groups ... as we mix with those of other beliefs ... as we learn to appreciate different cultures ... as the rigorous demands of today's stresses test us, if we make opportunity to name and appreciate our differences, I do believe we will also be a much stronger community.

Third, Prairie Sod isn't just aesthetically pleasing; it is good for grazing; it supports a reasonable balance of wild life; and it fosters gentle, life-giving water courses.

The reminder is that we learn to accept the limits of the gifts given to us. Don't over graze! Don't let the cattle make sump holes of the water springs! Don't force the land to produce more than it can handle! The truism is: "Look after the grass, and the grass will look after you."

We need to look after our communities in the same way. Don't be afraid to question whether or not constant economic expansion is wise. Don't be afraid to question whether or not you and your family need to be on the go every night. Ask yourselves what the cost is of not pay-ing a fair share to keep community health and education and social service Institutions viable.

Meditate and listen to the message given through a simple clump of sod.

We are gifted by God every day of our lives. Receive the gift with arms that are open, and with spirits that are willing to share. Take time to live prayerfully. And be prepared to be surprised by the riches that life offers.

For What We Are About

My aunt, at grace, would call the roll
of abstract blessings we possessed,
including the immortal soul
and chances for eternal rest.

My uncle, on the other hand,
would stress the weather and the wheat
and offer thanks for bottom land,
and what we were about to eat.

It struck me then as fairly clear
they had two different scales of worth,
but neither of them thought it queer
that one liked heaven, one the earth.
And though a small boy found it odd,
I doubt if it bewildered God.

Source Unknown

The Stippling

Any other woman in our neighbourhood would have offered to kill the two men, had they intruded in one of our homes. But Mary could always look beyond the mistakes to acknowledge the spirit of generosity in each person. All of us loved her, and many of us tried to become more forgiving because of her.

"Well! You know!" Mary told us in the overly loud voice of a partially deaf person, "You know, those boys meant well!" Her eyes sparkled as she told the story about the kindness of her middle aged friends.

Bill and Mary were a very hard working couple who farmed and raised cattle "out in the hills," twenty-five miles from town. When they weren't on horseback, working the livestock, they were weeding and hauling water to their orchard-like garden that miraculously survived our parched prairie conditions. Produce was carefully gathered and seed heads were saved, to be used next year. All these things were stored in boxes and piled in the porch of this extremely modest little home ... until there was only the narrowest of passage ways through to the kitchen.

But grandkids and company were always welcome. Visiting here was always an adventure. Bill would take your coat and scarf and whisk it away to a bedroom. Then, one after the other, our family would slide in along the bench to sit round in back of the kitchen table. There we would stay for the afternoon, laughing and talking as Bill stoked the fire and Mary whipped up a delicious chocolate cake. Huge pieces of it were eaten still hot, with ice cream melting on the dinner plate alongside .

... Back to the day the old couple came home to find the house in a mess, and two men passed out in the overstuffed chairs in the living room. These men were the local plasterers, and this was at the time when stippled ceilings were just becoming fashionable.

The men had stopped in for a drink and a visit. True, the folks weren't home, but their doors were never locked. So the men sat for a spell, poured themselves their drink, and mused over the generosity of these kind hearted folks. They decided it was time someone did a kind thing for them.

"Let's do their ceilings," one of the men volunteered. They had another drink to seal the contract, then set to work in the living room.

Obviously their senses were a bit clouded by this time. It didn't dawn on them that, when they wet the plaster board that was already on the ceiling, it would expand. Then, when they added the weight of the moist stipple plaster, the plaster board sagged everywhere except where it was held up with nails.

The men worked hard doing their good deed, toasted themselves when the work was done, sat down in the big chairs to admire their work, and fell sound asleep.

"Well! You know!" Mary repeated her favorite saying, "Those boys meant well! It used to be I had to sit up tall to look out the window at them there hills." (Mary had to stand on tiptoes to reach the five foot measure). "Now, I can just sit back in this big old chair and look up at my ceiling, and see the way it rolls between the nails... Not every one is as lucky as me!"

We were the lucky ones, we who spent many a Sunday afternoon in this home, with these special people.

This story reminds me of the words of the camp song that goes: *The Spirit in me greets the Spirit in you, Alleluia. God's in us, and we are in God. Alleluia!"*

Hidden Treasures

This true story illustrates what can happen when, as a community of people, we suddenly realize we are living under the rainbow of God's presence.

Some twenty years ago I was appointed as "The Saddle Bag Minister," and was expected to try to bring some quality of life back to a few dying communities in Southern Saskatchewan.

"Keeler" was the name of one of those communities. It had a hotel (which was really a bar), an old store and Post Office, a Community Hall, a small United Church that had stood empty for some time, and a population of 68 people. There was still a remnant of a church women's group, and they were keen to see if I could help them find some life in their old bones.

To make a long story short, I suggested we sponsor an Arts Festival because I had seen so many lovely examples of art and craft in the homes I had visited. We invited a couple of professional artists, booked a touring display of water-colour paintings, and invited a drama group from the city to put on a play. Then we spread the word, encouraging everyone from far and wide to bring their collections of buttons and arrowheads, their needle work and their polished rocks, their handmade jewelry and their wood carvings. Things worked into quite a fevered pitch - with more preparations going on in one day than had been evident in the past five years.

That afternoon, Mrs. Garry decided to take a break and walk from her little grocery store down to the Community Hall, "just to see what was doing." Her thick glasses were almost as smeared as the front windows of her old store. Long hours in the store had certainly taken their toll on her health ... She carefully looked at one display after another, muttering to herself and chatting with those setting up displays. Finally, she said, "I never would have thought of it ... Do you suppose I could bring a few pieces of my Chinaware?"

Come to find out, when Mrs. Garry first came to Keeler as a young bride, she busied herself painting yellow roses on fine bone Chinaware ... so delicate ... and oh so beautiful.

What a difference that moment made in how people looked at the rest of Mrs. Garry's life. Until then, she was only "poor old Mrs. Garry!," a woman behind a counter in a dingy little store in a dying town. But from that moment on the words was out. "Did you know Mrs. Garry painted? Have you ever seen such delicate work?"

It was like watching a butterfly burst free from the cocoon ... And as these people talked, the ones who once thought they could sum this woman up with a thimble full of words suddenly realized there was so much more to who she really was. The spirit of God's love flowed through the people. For a while they stopped constricting each other with outworn labels, and they looked at old acquaintances in new ways. There was a sense of joy and peace that felt so good!

Ezekiel's Valley of Dry Bones (Ezekiel 37)

I felt the powerful presence of the Lord, and his spirit took me and set me down in a valley where the ground was covered with bones. He led me all around the valley, and I could see that there were very many bones and that they were very dry. He said to me, "Mortal man, can these bones come back to life?"

I replied, "Sovereign Lord, only you can answer that!"

He said, "Prophesy to the bones. Tell these dry bones to listen to the word of the Lord. Tell them that I, the Sovereign Lord, am saying to them: I am going to put breath into you and bring you back to life. I will give you sinews and muscles, and cover you with skin. I will put breath into you and bring you back to life. Then you will know that I am the Lord."

So I prophesied as I had been told. While I was speaking, I heard a rattling noise, and the bones began to join together. While I watched, the bones were covered with sinews and muscles, and then with skin. But there was no breath in the bodies.

God said to me, "Mortal man, prophesy to the wind. Tell the wind that the Sovereign Lord commands it to come from every direction, to breathe into these dead bodies, and to bring them back to life."

So I prophesied as I had been told. Breath entered the bodies, and they came to life and stood up. There were enough of them to form an army.

God said to me, "Mortal man, the people ... are like these bones. They say that they are dried up, without any hope and with no future. So prophesy to my people ... and tell them that I, the Lord God, am going to open their graves ... I will put my breath in them, and bring them back to life ... I have promised that I would do this - and I will. I, the Lord, have spoken."

God's Rainbow
Paraphrase of Psalm 118:14 - 24

*For many people the skies above and the world of nature are like
theological textbooks revealing truths about God.*

God's rainbow arches over me; I fear nothing any more.
For what can conquer God?
Before the beginning, and after the end,
God is, and God will be.
Everything works together for God's goals.
If God is with me, nothing I do is wasted;
like sunbeams dancing on a lake, even my weakest efforts
will gather into the glory of God.
Gales may buffet me, and storm clouds may darken my face,
but God will never give up on me.

I will arise and go now;
I will sink into God's watery womb,
and rise again into a new life.
A new day has dawned.
God will look after me.
As a piece of driftwood becomes a work of art,
so God will find new uses for me.

Do not try to second-guess God,
for God is greater than all our imaginings.
This is the day God gave us -
rejoice and be glad in it.

by James Taylor

Carrying Comfort - In Comfort

One institution, the minister, does not change. Today, just as in the days of your childhood, he goes about, bringing cheer to the sick, comfort to the troubled, courage to the weak.

Week-days and Sunday his life is an active one. A problem that faces him is transportation. In another day, the horse and buggy was his only method of travel. Rough roads and weather of all sorts limited his capacity and accomplishment. He did all he could, but not all he would.

Today, appreciative congregations, sensitive to his word, at times under great handicap, have provided their minister with the most economical and dependable means of transportation - the FORD.

Ford Motor Cars are sturdily built. They have long life. They are low priced to buy and inexpensive to operate. Practical congregations have realized this fact. Your wisdom and kindly thoughtfulness can find concrete expression in supplying your minister with a Ford Car.

Today's car advertisements tell of the sporty toughness of a 4 x 4 that can crawl over unbelievably rugged terrain; or of the sleek, pulsating beauty of a body likened to a wild panther. But in the first volume of the United Church's "New Outlook" magazine, June 1, 1925 (the predecessor magazine to The Observer), the Ford Closed Car advertisement focuses on the needs and the role of the rural minister. This is a car that well serves one who moves with dignity, acts with dedication, and deserves the respect of the whole community. How could a congregation consider buying something of lesser value?

No Wolves Here!

When I take children with me, they know I'm not a parent. I expect
them to accept responsibilities for themselves. It is amazing to
watch how they work at living up to my expectations.

"Oh, I don't need to worry," Jimmie told his mom
when she asked what he should take for our overnight
camp out. "Joyce always has all the stuff we need."

I had invited eight boys to join me on a series of summer outings back into the Qu'Appelle Valley. First we
had a picnic. Next, we planned a cookout. With each
event, my plan was to have this group of nine-year-olds
learn a few more of the finer details of camping.

Now we were scheduled for our first sleepout. One of
the moms was to camp over with me. One of the dads
drove a truck load of gear up to the site we had chosen.
He would return to help us break camp first thing in the
morning.

As we watched the dust cloud from the retreating
truck, I overhead one small voice say to no one in particular "It's the first time I've ever camped without my
dad!" For we two women that was a signal that the boys
needed to get busy, and keep busy! Because of the hefty
breeze, we ordered the digging of one large fire pit, and
insisted there be no other fires until the wind died down
(usually as it got dark).

"You can set your tents up wherever you like," I told
them, "so long as you can still see the fire pit."
Immediately they moved out in pairs. Two boys moved
two hundred feet to the east, two boys moved two hundred and fifty feet to the west. Jimmie and his buddy
made their way down the slope to set their tent near a
clump of wolf willow. The other two boys decided to

move a bit further beyond them, "across the stream" (a trickle of water from an upper spring). They were going to "sleep under the stars"!

I found pleasure in watching how each pair tackled setting up camp. It was obvious they were enjoying their leisure. By seven o'clock they were all ready to cook their suppers over the central fire. We ate. We sang. We told stories. Slowly, the evening dusk started to settle, and it was time for all the boys to wend their way back toward their bed rolls.

I began to hear a bit of a nervous edge in Jimmie's voice. He looked back and forth between his tent and the central fire. "Joyce?" he quarried, "Have your got a flashlight?"

"Sure," I replied. "Didn't you bring yours?" That's when I remembered what his mom had told me about his casualness in preparing for our gathering. Furthermore, I knew the family always left one light on through the night because Jimmie didn't like the dark.

"Could I borrow your light?" he begged.

"Sure. I can loan it to you for a minute. But I'll need it back as soon as possible. After all, I'm responsible for the whole gang ... Better yet, let me hold the light on the trail for you till you get back to the tent."

"There are wolves in those bushes!" he pushed.

"Not wolves. Coyotes maybe!" I chuckled, "but no wolves ... Go on down and build up your fire now that the wind is down. Nothing will hurt you then." My compromise wasn't good enough ... "On the other hand, you could move your stuff up here, close to Dot and me, and closer to the fire ring."

Jimmie, and seven other boys were off like a flash ... Within twenty minutes, they were all huddled together, so close that some of the tent pegs were staked in the bare ground that was part of the fire pit. And even the guys who were "sleeping under the stars" found refuge under canvas ...

Next morning, after breakfast, as we pondered what we might have learned from this experience, one thing was abundantly clear. "We know why the wagons camped in circles each night ... Ya! The world looks a whole lot different in the dark!"

... By the end of the summer our boys learned to handle themselves pretty well. We enjoyed many hours of hiking, camping, exploring the beauty hidden in our prairie world, and finding the strengths hidden in ourselves.

Long Live Our Differences

Too often organizers of a particular event think all of their speakers should be selected because they share a particular mind set. Let us tell you what happened when two very different, very stubborn women were forced to work together!

There's a difference of one generation between Elsie and me. It is evident not only when you look at our ages, but also when you discuss our theology. This difference was particularly evident when it came to interpreting our mission field experience.

We had both been invited to work with the Presbyterian Church in the Republic of Korea. We were both there at the same time, though Elsie had already spent a number of years there when I arrived. And both of us worked in the rural regions of the Hermit Kingdom.

So I guess it was only natural, since we returned to Canada to live in the same city, that we would both be invited to "speak" at a local Mission Festival. The problem was that, because of our differences and our unwillingness to compromise our understandings of mission, we firmly believed we shouldn't appear on the same venue together.

We invited the organizer for the event to lunch, explained how different our thinking was, affirmed that neither of us would defer to the other's point of view (even though we respected the other person for what she had to say), ... and insisted that the organizer choose one or the other of us as the guest speaker.

"Thanks for the lunch," our organizer friend declared. "Now, I'll expect both of you to be at the program Saturday evening. What you do with the time we've given on the program is up to you. But I want to have both of you attend our event. And I want both of you to be part of the presentation.

Avoidance of a difficult situation, as they say, is the easiest way out. Our friend Malcolm closed the door on that option. It was now up to us to work through to our own solution.

Inspiration struck. One of us would choose the 35 mm slides that we would show. The other would do the commentary!

We were much more nervous than usual that evening. Both of us wanted to present our own theological interpretation of how we understood the mission of the church. Yet neither of us wanted to polarize the discussion, or appear to be quarrelsome.

The dark clouds of controversy that loomed in our thinking were soon diminished. We each talked freely about our understandings ... and our differences. By the end of the evening I came to realize what strength there was in honestly sharing our differences. All of us were truly enlightened.

Most of the audience already knew us as two very different individuals. They appreciated our struggles to speak out of our own understanding. They enjoyed the humour, the edge of controversy, the sense of vitality that undergirded our discussion.

Ultimately all of us realized that such differences are normal, and that it is important to give the individuals in the audience freedom to do their own thinking, and freedom to draw their own conclusions.

Ever since that time I have often encouraged people to publicly yet respectfully share their differences. That way no one in the audience has the excuse of needing to catch up on "40 winks."

Carl Dudley understood this when he wrote his comments about people in a small church relating with each other. One of his points was that "each person (in the small church) is accepted, not equally, but individually, by name." He also noted the following:

"In a big world, the small church has remained intimate.
In a fast world, the small church has been steady.
In an expensive world, the small church has remained plain.
In a complex world, the small church has remained simple.
In a rational world, the small church has kept feelings.
In a mobile world, the small church has been an anchor.
In an anonymous world, the small church calls us by name - by nickname!
As a result, the small church has survived where others have failed."

Making The Small Church Effective, by Carl Dudley

The Burmis Tree

The "Burmis Tree," a limber pine, is a landmark that is located off Highway # 3, near the entrance to the Crowsnest Pass. It was particularly poignant to share this meditation with long-time residents in the area. Many with tears in their eyes later told me memories of their association with the tree.

It is interesting to find that something that has been dead for at least fifteen years should be the thing that gives hope to anyone. But that is what the Burmis Tree does for me.

When I learn that trees of this species live more than three hundred years, I marvel at how many storms this one has withstood. When I think about its smallness, I wonder how it has remained so tenacious and strong. Probably it is because it does not impose itself on the world around. When I was told about its inherent flexibility and resilience, I better understood how it stood up to the rigors of those branch-breaking gales. Evidently the branches of this kind of pine can be tied in knots without breaking. The short lance-shaped needles help conserve water. That is how it is specially adapted to withstand drought and starvation. And I have waited for this old landmark to fall over, as do lodge pole pines. But these rugged, tough little mavericks of the mountain slopes have such deep tap roots that they are kept securely in place for centuries.

The Burmis Tree is so homely, that even the lumber men pass it by. It is so old, it witnessed the birth of all life around it. It is so stunted, it arrests the attention of everyone who drives the highway. What better symbol of life amid this rugged, wind-tortured land? What better symbol of hope in time of rigorous economic, political and social upheaval, and in times of mind-boggling change?

The Spirit of the Tree speaks to us of life, even while we see it in death. The Symbol of the Tree reminds us of the importance of roots that are strong, and of the need for a resilience that is limber. I remember that the God who created the Burmis Tree, and its brothers and sisters, is the God who created us. I remember that the God who stood beside the Burmis Tree through drought and gale, is the God who stands beside us in our times of testing. I remember that the God who gave the Burmis tree the spirit and will to endure, is the God who has given us strength beyond our own strength, and the will to endure under the harshest circumstances.

The Psalmist of old must surely have witnessed similar scenes of courage under rigorous testing. For, with assurance and confidence, he wrote:

"Therefore, we will not fear, though the earth be removed, and though the mountains be carried into the midst of the sea!" (Psalm 46:2)

Even as the old Burmis Tree stands stark and naked on the mountain slope, it offers the gift of shelter and life to the tiny animals hiding in its roots. In death, it still has

life. The sense of security we have because we know
our spiritual roots gives us a strong anchor. We are freed
to reach out with open arms to others. Hence we are
able to offer our own gifts of compassion and love.

To Volunteer, or Not To Volunteer

*Volunteer Committee work is essential to the life of any rural com-
munity. But it is never easy. Volunteers often feel the searing bite
of criticism, and the sharp crack of tongue lashings. Some ask "Why
bother?" Others wisely carry on because they feel there is a job that
needs to be done despite the criticism. In the end, a good laugh
often clears the air over the extremes of a particular grumble... And
the faithful carry on.*

Obviously there had been a break down in communication, and I had some very distraught people on the
phone. Now it was up to me to give some leadership. I
could either dump the problem back in my callers' laps
... or I could recognize this as one of those teachable
moments.

I was, at that time, the Saddle Bag Minister. And our
rural experimental project needed a major cash infusion.
We decided to hold a community auction sale. That
involved canvassing for saleable items, soliciting the
generous support of a local auctioneer, and advertising
the event far and wide.

One of the novice members of our Board farmed
down the road from the local auctioneer. She offered to
approach this man and ask him to volunteer his services
for our sale. Unfortunately, since we talked about needing to start promoting our event immediately, everyone
assumed this contact would be made within the next
twenty-four hours.

The Advertising Committee immediately geared themselves for action. Within a very short time promotional posters were designed, printed, and distributed throughout the region ... with the auctioneer's name bannered across the bottom of each poster.

Alas, talking with the guy down the road doesn't always happen as quickly as it might. By the time the two neighbors did talk, the auctioneer had already seen a poster, and was angry at our presumptuousness! He was offended, and was in no mood to fill his role. We would simply have to carry on without his help!

What to do? Our idealistic young committee member dissolved into tears. Her self-esteem was shattered. She was ready to bail out of the entire project. She never wanted to do anything for anybody again. Committee work was verboten!

She wailed as she told her side of the story. She sobbed as she told of her repeated attempt to meet with him, to apologize and try to set things right.

"Stop right there", I insisted. "Stop, and listen to me. You have done what you could. You have done it as best you could. You weren't the only one to goof. Now you need to hand your problem over to someone else on the Committee. That is why we have a committee in the first place ... so we can help each other, and so we can complement each others' abilities with what we have to offer."

I got her to stop her wailing long enough to help me decide who could best approach the offended auctioneer. We wanted someone who could give voice to her apology ... who would probably say, "You know how it is when you are young and inexperienced ... Slip-ups happen ... She didn't know it was so important to get to you immediately ... And the others didn't know they had to

wait to get confirmation before printing their posters ..."
We needed someone who could tell him we all meant
well ... We weren't being presumptuous ... And we
would appreciate his cooperation
   "Now," I advised, "Phone Les and Mary (an older
couple on our committee) ... explain your predicament,
and ask for their help. Tell them what you have told me.
Tell them about the impossible situation as you see it.
Let them know how badly you feel ... and how much you
want to mend fences ... Then trust they will do the rest."
   Not only did I feel it important to get the differences
sorted out between neighbors who would likely be farm-
ing side-by-side for the rest of their lives, but I also
wanted to take advantage of this teachable moment to
tell my young idealist that committee work is never clear
sailing. Always the personalities, the power struggles,
the bruised egos, and the simple breakdowns in communication lurk on the the fringes of any committee project.
I showed her how to learn to anticipate where she could,
and how to learn to keep her cool when she must.
Above all, I showed her how to seek out the special con-
tributions each committee member could offer, and how
to invite the cooperation of all for the good of the whole.

Post Script:

Les and Mary did make their visit to the auctioneer's
home. Over coffee, and after they had talked about the
weather and the price of wheat, eventually they spoke
about the primary reason for their visit. They talked
about how important the auction was. They talked about
how much all the younger members of the committee
were learning about working together ... And how much
the oldsters appreciated the young people's enthusiasm
and involvement. They passed on the apology their

young friend and others on the committee wished them to convey ... And they invited the young auctioneer to reconsider his response. His generosity would mean so much to the success of our project.

The auctioneer accepted the apology and the invitation. Everyone saved face. Everyone grew a little taller for having worked through this tough situation. The community was made stronger because we took the time to work things through.

... And bye-the-bye, the actual sale was a great success!

On The Right Track?

On the vast open fields of the Canadian Prairies, every farmer longs, above all else, to plough straight furrows, and plant straight rows of grain or grass. If not, he is razzed by his neighbors for the rest of the season.

So you can imagine the consternation of one farmer when the seeded rows in his field drifted off in a maze of unsightly directions. He had carefully instructed the new hired man to find some kind of a marker in the distance and fix his eyes on it as he drove down the field. "When you make that first round," he said, "keep your eye on that marker and drive toward it. That way, you will keep going straight."

After letting off some considerable steam regarding the stupidity of the new hired hand, he concluded with "What the hell were you watching, anyhow?"

The man's reply: "A cloud!"

Farm Auction

It is so heartbreaking -
   That's the way I feel about farm auctions.
Collections ... memories of a lifetime laid bare before
an audience.
      Half are lusting for a bargain
      Half are aching as yet another farm changes hands

Men come in their half-tons and feed trucks.
   They buy log chains, buckets of bolts, and old harness
      as they contemplate what their bid might be
      on the harrows or the tractor.

Women gather around the household furnishings and
"the rack" -
   Watching, waiting ...
      trying to hold their head rigid while answering a
      neighbor's query.
   They love the boxes of doilies and fancy linen.
   They want kitchen ware for their son's new apartment.

Children run freely back and forth between the
concession stand
   and the rail fence where they can climb, hang by their shins,
   and dare a new acquaintance to do better.

Those who make a business of collecting
   act as casual and indifferent as possible.
But the locals know who they are,
   and bid the prices up to assure the seller gets a fair deal.

Weeks have been spent sorting and discarding,
   repairing and painting major pieces of machinery.
Memories come back of the sacrifice made to purchase this,

the time we got stuck in the mud while using that,
or how someone long gone suggested we might
make an improvement
by welding a support bar across a particular weak spot.

Against the rhythm of the auction patter
they talk about the cost of machinery
and the price of livestock ...
and what another rain would do for the hay.

Women from a district organization set up a lunch
booth in the shed.
All they need are a couple of plug ins for their big
coffee urns,
some camp stoves to heat the bar-b-que beef,
and a generous supply of doughnuts, chocolate bars,
and canned pop.
It's a profitable afternoon.

In the big house the elders gather, to talk over other
times and sales,
and to help each other get through the day.

By nightfall, bone weary from hard work and suppressed
emotion,
the principals take their faithful helpers to supper in town.
Too tired to eat...
Too choked to express their gratitude ...
the conversation lingers between dry jokes,
bits of news about who they did or didn't see ...
and how glad they are that it's all behind them.

Tomorrow will come!
Tomorrow they will get on with the rest of their lives!

My Father Johnny Green
by his son Jim

My old man
he had a grocery store
trimming lettuce every morning
stamping cans for years
    never was a grocer.
He ran a meat market
cutting meat till his hands
were raw and sore
wrestling with rump roasts
    never was a butcher.

My old man
with his bent straw hat
blue Players tobacco can
creel full of fresh trout
waders flapping when he ran
    he was a born fisherman.

First fish he ever showed to me
long hairy arm aiming down
into the shifting shadows of the Highwood River
I didn't see them right away.
    It was that night in a panavision dream
    I saw those daring phantom shapes
    hanging around in that boiling stream
        lifting   rising
            sinking   diving
    Eerie underwater people
    in a world all new to me.

I hung around the flagpole in the back yard
watching silver scales hit the old wash tub.
I felt the whitefish smell in my nose
heard the knife scraping as she goes.
From broom handles and bright house paint
he made doubled-jointed casting plugs.
From a broken black rod, a tip, and solder
he made my first and proudest fishing pole.

We'd wade the tumbling mountain creeks
my old man, my brothers and me.
Sometimes he'd hand me his rod and say
    "hold this"
and right away I'd catch a fish.
    "Keep that line tight," He'd say
and let me land or lose
the battling trout we knew he'd hooked.

I can see my old man down on his knees
crawling through the dry late summer grass
hunting grasshoppers with a rolled up newspaper
stopping to hold up a fat one
    "Look at that little beggar," he'd say
    "green all over"
then he'd tuck it in the Players can
with the holes punched in the top.

Nights we'd sit around the campfire
or the oil cloth covered table at the ranch
by the yellow light of the kerosene lamp
eating beans and laughing and talking fish
talking about tomorrow.

My old man
he took us after muskie,
out to Fish Lake for pike,
he taught us to troll for lunkers,
and where to find minnows for bait.
We waded streams for brookies
and crept the creeks for rainbow.
It took a lot of years these things
because we had a lot to learn.
Miles of line were wet back then
and scores of cook fires burned.

My old man
the fisherman
          he was a Father.

There came a day when I left home.
Dave's turn came and he went west to go to school.
Bob worked in the store for a time and fished with Dad.
Jerry had to leave town to learn a trade
before he came back to stay with Dad.
So we scattered out and would come back together
to go fishing and talking and remembering back
to how things used to be when we were kids
and how things never stay the same
but shift and change like the shapes of clouds.

And sure enough things have changed again -
But my brothers and I don't think of Dad as dead and gone.
He's just out there ahead of us like he always was
scouting new territory, getting the lay of the land
and by the time we catch up to him
he'll have all the trails down pat

and all the hidden pools located,
even be able to caution us where to walk.

And that's it -

Dad's out there ahead of us
blazing the trail for his sons
just like he always did.
Except now he's breaking trail
for grandsons and a granddaughter too
because that's what Fathers
        and Grandfathers do.

Experiencing the Pain

Tongue Creek Church

As people drive through the countryside, they can't help but notice the comfortable farm homes, the big cars, and the huge farm equipment. No wonder they jump to the conclusion that "all is well!"

It is only as one gets closer, takes time to hang around the local cafe or the seniors drop-in center, that a different story starts to appear. Beyond the brave front put on by those who pretend their neighbors don't know what's happening, there unfold stories of hardship and pain.

That pain is always with us, for country living is never easy. Still, we go back to the land, and the small towns, and the villages, because that is where we belong. Many of us have lived elsewhere ... But we return, content with the knowledge that there is no Promised Land, except where we choose to make one.

In Time of Community Crisis
Prayer Opening The Service of Worship

Tragedy has come into the midst of our community
this week,
O God, and we have difficulty knowing what to think,
what to say,
what to do.
>> We pray for wisdom and guidance.
>> We pray for mercy and compassion.
>> We pray for the will to do what is right ...
>> and the desire to turn away from what is expedient.
> We pray that, as a Faith Community,
>> we can reach out to each other
>> in ways that show Christ-like caring.
> These things we pray in Jesus' name.   Amen

We Can Grow Strong
... Even In The Broken Places

None of us comes from a home that has not known sorrow ...
All of us have had some experience with knowing what
it is like to be hurt by life -
> We have known anguish because of sickness and death ...
> We have been tormented by broken promises
> and shattered dreams ...
> We have been torn apart by tragedies that are
> sometimes of our own doing ...
> We even grow cynical and curse God for letting
> things happen to us ...

But again and again our Gospel stops us there ...
 It shows us that ours is a merciful and compassionate God.
It reminds us that we are often more critical and judgmental of each other
than seems reasonable for those trying to lead godly lives.
   It calls us to own up to our own weaknesses and
   shortcomings ...
   then trust ourselves into the hands of a merciful God.

It is so easy to get caught up in doing what is most popular ...
or what appears to be most apparent at the time ...
   But the true Gospel invites us to pause first, in prayerful contemplation,
   then act according to God's calling ...
   to bring healing from a strength beyond ourselves.

Those who trust in the Lord for help
  will find their strength renewed.
They will rise on wings like eagles;
  They will run and not
  get weary.
  They will walk and
  not grow weak.

Isaiah 40:31

J. CANTELON

Confessional
(Paraphrase of Psalm 32)

It feels good to confess something and clear it from your conscience.
After that, it is easier to taste freedom, feel strengthened, and start
noticing life's blessings.

Happy are those who have nothing to hide;
Even happier those whose slate has been wiped clean.
I used to lie awake, worrying about things I had done;
and during the day, about things I had not done.
My conscience tormented me, I couldn't concentrate.
I was terrified of being exposed.

So I went to God, and confessed.
I made no excuses for myself; I didn't hide anything.
And God forgave me .
What a relief it is to share a gnawing secret!
Forgiveness is like a cool drink on a hot day,
like a warm fire in a winter blizzard.
God's grace renews my strength;
It gives me a second chance.

God says "I will teach you how to take charge of your
behaviour.
You are not like horses and camels
who need bridles and bits to control them.
You have a mind; you can think,
You can anticipate consequences before you act."
Experience isn't always the best teacher.
Let God lead you through life.

by James Taylor

An Ancient Legend

There was a man in the land of Uz, whose name was Job;
And that man was blameless and upright, one who
feared God, and turned away from evil.
There were born to him seven sons and three daughters.
He had seven thousand sheep, three thousand camels,
five hundred yoke of oxen, and five hundred she asses,
and very many servants; so that this man was
greatest of all the people of the east.

His sons used to go and hold a feast in the house of
each on his day; and they would send and invite
their three sisters to eat and drink with them.
And when the days of the feast had run their
course, Job would send and sanctify them.
And he would rise early in the morning and offer
burnt offerings according to the number of them all;
for Job said, 'It may be that my sons have sinned and
cursed God in their hearts.'
Thus Job did continually.   *Job 1:1-5*

A Modern Application of Ancient Truths

Many a parent is like Job, the Old Testament Patriarch, who is overly generous in doing what he can for his kids. But Job learns that it doesn't help to try to do everything on behalf of his children. To acquire wisdom and understanding, each individual must have his or her own experience of God.

I appreciate this story because I had a father who was always making sacrifices on my behalf. We didn't have much money in the early Forties, but, "By hell," he would say, working into the night, "I never had a bike, and I'm going to make sure my kids have a bike!" Time and again he did for us, giving up something of his on our behalf to try to make it easier for us as we grew up.

I see so many parents doing the same thing today - giving the kids more money than the parents can afford. They turn over to the kids a vehicle because of peer pressure (on both parent and child). They cover for the kids' mistakes when it might be better for them to learn from the consequences ... They even stand before the Creator in the place of the children, as did Job, fearful "lest one of them sinned or cursed God in his heart."

It is important that we look closely at the rest of the Job story. Job went through all the right moves. He prayed. He offered sacrifices. He was more than generous with his kids ... He acted in accord with the predominant understandings of his day ... But the story of Job is really a story about the difference there is between having knowledge and using wisdom. Job was well informed about how to intercede before God of his family's behalf. But whether or not that knowledge was enough to help Job make wise decisions would only be seen later.

Wisdom came when the man, with all his knowledge, was put to the test. He faced every kind of cruel, unthinkable test. His kids were killed! He went through bankruptcy! His health gave out! He was humiliated in every way! Another person might have broken under the weight of despair ... But Job held on. Out of the depth of his own being he sensed that he was being forced to reach beyond himself. He found there was something more to life than having the pat answers as to how to make things easier for those you love. Wisdom came with searching out the spiritual truths. Wisdom came with taking time for reflection. Wisdom came with listening for the voice of One who was greater.

At the conclusion of the story, Job recognized himself to be a wiser person. He had walked the walk. He had lived through and reached beyond the pain. Instead of trying to live up to the expectations of others, he caught a first hand glimpse of the Almighty.

Now, because he felt this relationship, Job was able to say to the Creator:

I know that thou canst do all things
  and that no purpose of thine can be thwarted ...
(In the past) I have uttered what I did not understand,
  things too wonderful for me, which I did not know ...
(Now I understand out of my own experience).
I had heard of thee by the hearing of the ear,
  but now my eye sees thee. (I stand in relationship with thee),
  And I repent (of my past).   Job 42:1-6

Then it was, according to the story teller, that Job lived out the rest of his life as a happier and a wiser person.

In our own day, parents and teachers and coaches may do everything they can to intervene on our behalf ... Internet and technology may bring us more information than we can ever handle ... But it is only in our own search after wisdom and understanding that we will find our personal peace.

Walking Wounded

The Apostle Paul faced all sorts of difficulties. He had physical affirmances. He was punished with whippings and imprisonment. In his travels he experienced ship wrecks, robberies, and accusations by false friends. After listing these things, he tells us about seeking release. He asked God to make his life easier. Then he heard God say, "My grace is all you need. My power is strongest when you are weak." (2 Corinthians 2:7-10)

Several years ago, at a Mother's Day service, I gave a family prayer in which I prayed for all the hurting families in our small village. In categories, I mentioned families who were hurt because of separation or divorce, parents who had to raise their children as single parents, and grandparents who had to now raise a generation of grandchildren.

Barely did I get through my lunch that afternoon, when one of the community matriarchs came banging on my door.

"You know, Sasse," she said as I opened the door, "I sure thought you had blown it this morning with that prayer of yours!" I tried to invite this obviously upset woman into the house, but she seemed to need to get something more off her chest right there at the door!

"Usually you seem to be pretty tuned in to what's happening in our community, but this time I thought you were really off-base. Still, you made me think ... I have to admit, I never heard the rest of your service. I did a lot of thinking about our own family situation ... and about all the other families that were sitting in church with me!"

My friend went on to point out that most of the families at church that morning were "old families" in what was both an established rural community and a bedroom village. She realized that every family in that church was touched by divorce, or separation, or they had children born to single mothers, or they were grandparents doing what they could to care for little ones.

"These are things we don't talk about with each other," she said. "So I thought, at first, that ours was the only family that was upset in this way. But Sasse you were right! We've got to stop carrying this as our silent burden. It's killing us ... We are withdrawing from each other ... We are hiding our feelings from each other, just when we need each other most!"

Having purged herself of her dismay at realizing these things, my friend then came in, and we talked through the afternoon. We talked about her feelings over the way all three of her children were divorced from their spouses. We talked about the feelings she shared with her husband, that somehow they had failed their kids. They wondered if maybe they were being punished or judged for something from the past. She talked about how she felt it her responsibility, each summer and at holiday time, to have the grandchildren home - to give her single, working daughter a bit of a breather! She talked a lot about the broken expectations she had ... that their family would be a model for others in the community to follow. But circumstances and decisions beyond her control made her feel like a failure in the eyes of the community. That is why she hadn't been able to give voice to these things, even when she knew other families faced similar crises...

This is a story too many of us can relate to because of our own situation. We have feelings of failure ... and of getting trapped in something not of our own choosing. We desperately try to survive, but often feel strung out to the end of our wits. Our nerves are frayed, and often there seems to be no sense of hope. And above all, there is the code of silence ... the code that suggests this is "our" problem, and "ours alone!"

As we talked, my friend indicated that, already, she started to feel better. For one thing, she realized it wasn't her responsibility to judge herself nor her children so harshly. That, of itself, gave her a little sense of freedom. Her feeling of self worth wasn't under the gun!

Second, it helped to talk about things she had bottled inside for so long. That was when she started thinking about her friend who had discovered (only last month) that their son was facing a major crisis in his family ... Now, my friend began to realize that possibly giving a listening ear and a compassionate shoulder to another person, of itself, was the gift she had to offer.

As we talked about how many children in our nearest school came from families that had faced severe disruption, we even got to thinking about how we, as a church, could reach out to the rest of the community. The prayer at church was only a starter, but it gave us an excuse to talk with each other. Could we look at having other discussion groups ... of forming support networks ... of helping parents improve their parenting skills ... of having a "Marriage Enrichment" program for couples ... of offering something to help grandparents who had to start over with a new generation ...

That discussion actually did happen some time ago, in a place some distance from where I am today. But it might as easily have happened yesterday, right in the middle of any of our communities. I tell you about it now because I suspect that every one of our families, in one way or another, have been touched by these same kind of circumstances. The problem of the breakdown of traditional family patterns continues ... and so does the atmosphere of frustration ... and guilt ... and silence!

Were we to open a discussion about our wounds, and were we to talk about the places where we hurt the worst, I suspect these are the feelings of frustration and pain that we would be least likely to put into words. They would be, "the sighs that are too deep for words." (Romans 8:27) It is comforting to know that God sees into our hearts, and helps us share glimpses of ourselves with others.

Prayer

O God, life is often so overwhelming, we hardly know where to turn. We wrap our wings around ourselves and try to hide from the painful and difficult times that threaten us.

But we feel you constantly calling out to encourage us, and enable us. We know that you are with us, reminding us that it is as we share with others, that we ourselves receive so many gifts. Teach us how to put our most overwhelming fears and doubts into words. Help us give expression to our grief and our anger. Show us how to pray for others, not with empty words, but with meaningful actions. Direct us to look always for the light and love of your presence.

It is as we say these things that we pray for the sick and the lonely and the dying. We pray in Jesus' name. Amen.

Kitchen Changes

*Oft times one generation disappoints another. It doesn't happen by
intention. But everyone is aware of a very real hurt.*

It happens to each of us at one time or another.
Change, that is. Changes that we didn't ask for.
Changes that we aren't sure we like!

It happened to me right there at the doorway of our
big farm kitchen. My folks had worked hard for a week
before I came home from the city ... and they had been at
it until 3 A.M. the day I arrived, trying to finish laying
the floor tile.

I knew as soon as I stepped off the bus that something
was up. Usually we stopped at the grocery store, and
visited at my aunt's, and dropped round to pick up the
mail. But this time it was off the Greyhound, into the
car, out to the farm ... Just like that!

They kicked their boots off in the porch, and pushed
into the kitchen ahead of me. Both Mom and Dad had
grins so broad they could have swallowed a watermelon
- whole.

"Well?" they asked, waiting for my reaction. "Well,
what do you think?"

What I thought, and what I felt, and what I said where
all separated by extended hesitations. I thought about
the daring ... the planning ... the wanting to surprise me,
as I had so often wanted to surprise them. The black
rings under their eyes told a good deal of the story. They
worked so hard. They did so much. But they had done
nothing to prepare me ... Our enormous, sparkling white
kitchen, which had always been the centre of our farm
and our family, was gone! In its place I saw turquoise

cupboards with pink doors, and slate gray tiles on the floor. It was the latest in designer kitchens ... but it wasn't my home. I could only swallow hard and acknowledge their efforts with a gulp of air. It would take time for the shock to pass. Truly, I was sorry I couldn't ooze the enthusiasm my parents expected. It was too much too fast ... However, I hope I'm a wiser person because of that experience.

In my own attempt to initiate change I now recognize how important it is to help people talk about the possibilities of change ... anticipate change ... sample a few ways of accomplishing change ... consider the alternatives. Above all, I never want to threaten folks with the implication that these changes need to be in place forever.

Dance Little Jean

A most fitting rainbow story. Sung by the Nitty Gritty Dirt Band.

The song starts out with all the storm clouds one can imagine. A musician who has been hired to play for a wedding dance isn't very keen on weddings. He is timid because he, himself, has been hurt for daring to love. These two people getting married, he expects they don't have a clue as to "what's in store after their honeymoon." In the background there is a girl child, born out of wedlock, who has spent so much in the way of "years and tears and sad confusion" ... until this very day.

Then something wonderful happens. Against the blackness of the thunderhead, the musician casts some light with the beat of his song, and a tiny rainbow appears... then another ... and another ... all because of

"Little Jean."

Can't you imagine how ecstatic this child is on this day, "When her mom marries her dad!" Can't you see yourself there on the edge of the dance floor, when Little Jean begins to whirl and twirl, "her crinoline billowing beneath her calico skirt!" Can't you imagine joy electrifying the whole crowd as they see her joy ... As they remember her prayers that this might happen! Can't you imagine the clapping! the laughing! the stomping! the music that played on and on for this happy Little Jean!

"Dance Little Jean, this day is for you.
Two people you love stood up to say 'I do'.
Dance little Jean. The prayer that you had
Was answered today. Your mama's marrying your dad!"

I see rainbows reflecting from the shining faces and the radiant hearts of so many in the dance-floor image ... And I sense those rainbows gave a glow of hope to all who would leave that celebration with a warm memory tucked close inside ... "Dance, Little Jean!"

I played at a wedding for the money,
and I wished I could have told the bride and groom
just what I think of marriage,
what's in store after their honeymoon.
And I was grumbling to the dancers
about how men and women all live apart,
and how a promise never made
cannot be broken, and can never break a heart.

Then suddenly from out of nowhere
a little girl came dancing across the floor,
her crinoline a billowing

beneath the skirt of calico she wore.
I saw all the joy of all the honored guests
as each of them was dying to let free.
They laughed and stomped, and clapped their hands
and hollered at her "Dance, little Jean!"
"Dance little Jean, this day is for you.
Two people you love stood up to say 'I do'.
Dance little Jean, the prayer that you had
was answered today. Your mama's marrying your dad."

My cynical heart just melted
as I figured what this get-together meant,
and how many tears and years and sad confusion
that little girl had spent.
Then he told the band to pack it up
about the time the couple cut the cake,
but we played as long as they stayed -
for love and laughs, for little Jeanie's sake.
She was a happy little girl,
and we played, "Dance, little Jean!"
"Dance little Jean, this day is for you.
Two people you love stood up to say 'I do.'
Dance little Jean. The prayer that you had
was answered today. Your mama's marrying your dad."

The Closest Companion
Paraphrase of Psalm 121

Advice uttered three thousand years ago by Middle Eastern sages,
but cloaked in contemporary images, helps again to give support to
our everyday lives.

Let others seek their gods in the executive suite;
let them put their faith in rising to the top.

We know where our help comes from;
it comes from the one who made heaven and earth.
Our God watches over every aspect of creation.
As a doting parent tends a toddler,
God holds out a hand when we stumble;
God will not let us fall down the stairs
before we have learned to walk on our own.
God does not play off one person against another.
God has no favorites;
God never tires of caring.
no crisis can destroy you;
though you lose loved ones, career, or health,
if you retain your relationship with God,
you will not be embittered;
you can emerge from the pain a better person.
Wherever you go, whatever you do,
God will go with you.

by James Taylor

Healing Possibilities

*The following is a tragic, haunting story, full of grief and pain. But
I share it with you, as a friend shared it with me, because of the
important signal of healing and hope that comes at the end. As a
people who believe that life carries on, even in the midst of death,
we need to hear how others have shared their message of hope in
the midst of very tragic circumstances.*

The story begins with a couple of youngsters forcing
their way into the locked gun cupboard in their home.
Boys being boys, they grabbed a gun and started playing
with it. The gun went off, and the twelve year-old was

shot in the head!

To make a long story short, he was rushed off by ambulance to the nearest hospital. Parents and a distraught eleven year old followed in the car. But, when a sign outside the Intensive Care Unit at the hospital read, "Children under twelve not allowed," the upset father couldn't think of anything else to do but put the eleven year old in a taxi, give him some money and the house key ... and send him back home. They assured him they would be there as soon as possible!

A few moments later, the doctor came in to tell the parents there was no hope for their stricken son. That doctor also informed the couple that the Palliative Care Nurse had been called, and would be with them in a moment.

Imagine, if you can what was in the mind of that nurse as she answered her call! In the midst of such tragedy, what came first?

She grabbed a phone, called the police and ordered them to go to the house, pick up the eleven year old, and bring him directly to her. Moments later the lad arrived in a state of absolute shock ... eyes glazed ... scared of the police ...unable to comprehend anything! The nurse grabbed him by the collar of his jacket, shook him and shouted at him again and again. "We'll get through this together!" "Hear me." "We'll do it!"

She repeated the action several times, till she saw the glaze lift slightly ... Then she took him into the Care Unit, to his brother's bedside. She took the hand of the one brother, and placed it in the hand of the other. Then she insisted that the younger boy talk to his brother. Calmly but firmly she repeated her command. Finally, as she paused for breath, she heard him say ever so faintly, "I'm sorry! ... I'm sorry!" And he started to cry. With the tears, more words came, words that needed to be said!

That nurse knew she could not allow the younger boy to carry his silent load of guilt for the rest of his days. Because of what she did, in reality she saved his life. Her caring, her actions, her understanding made all the difference to the quality of his life. At that moment, in a very real sense the healing process was begun. In the midst of a seemingly impossible situation it WAS possible to do something!

Hopefully we will never find ourselves in her situation, but often we can still follow her lead if we have unresolved agonies in our own lives, or if we know of others who feel they cannot reach back beyond the pall of death. A letter, ... thoughts expressed prayerfully, ... talking through a puppet, ... we need to search out ways to give voice to those yet unsaid feelings that can otherwise darken the rest of our lives.

Misunderstanding

Too often the gulf between urban and rural ways of thinking is like a chasm ... and some refuse to chance the crossing.

Not only was Tanya the new minister's wife. She was also a new bride. And she was new to small town living.

My first inkling of trouble came in mid-November when Tanya told us, at a gathering of neighboring clergy, what happened a couple of weeks previous. She could only label the incident as one of people being totally "insensitive" and blatantly "presumptuous."

The time had come for the annual fall supper ... a

major fund raiser and community builder for the congregation. "Can you imagine it?" Tanya wailed, a high level of emotion still in her voice. "Two of those women appeared at my door with a recipe, and a bag of carrots and cabbage, to tell me ... TELL ME ... that I could make the cabbage salad for whatever it was that they were having!"

Her husband sympathetically rested his hand on her arm to try to comfort her. But Tanya wasn't about to be comforted. She had never had anything like this done to her in the comfortable Toronto suburb where she had been raised.

My heart bled both for her ... and for the members of that UCW group. I could imagine part of the discussion the planning committee for the Smorgasbord Event would have had as they hitched themselves into action. They wanted to be sure to include the new minister's wife, although they knew she wasn't long on cooking experience. They had probably debated these matters for some time. Finally, someone came up with a fail-proof plan. No one had ever goofed yet on the old cabbage slaw with oil and vinegar dressing. Besides, there was lots of cabbage and carrots freshly gathered from gardens in the community. They would be glad to provide her with the makings. This gave a couple of members a chance to pay a visit and help her find her way.

... Tanya absolutely refused to do what the parishioners asked. Her one role was to attend the supper on the arm of her husband, The Minister!

The two different worlds of understanding never did find a common ground. Within 12 months the young couple announced they were leaving, to go overseas for further studies. My heart ached as I thought about the many walls that divide people from each other.

Hymn: The Servant Song

For six months we sang verses three to five of this hymn as a dedi-
cation prayer when our offering was presented on Sunday morning.
Each week the imagery in the words opened new doors for me.

Sister, let me be your servant,
let me be as Christ to you;
pray that I may have the grace
to let you be my servant too.

We are pilgrims on a journey,
fellow travellers on the road;
we are here to help each other
walk the mile and bear the load.

I will hold the Christ-light for you
in the nighttime of your fear;
I will hold my hand out to you,
speak the peace you long to hear.

I will weep when you are weeping,
when you laugh I'll laugh with you;
I will share your joy and sorrow,
till we've seen this journey thro'.

When we sing to God in heaven,
we shall find such harmony,
born of all we've known together
of Christ's love and agony.

Brother, let me be your servant,
let me be as Christ to you;
pray that I may have the grace
to let you be my servant too.

by Richard Gilliard

The Thoughtfulness Of A Child

The capacity to express kindness and love is found in every age group.

Ashley was 5 years old when her mother's nerves gave out. It had been a roller-coaster year for the whole family. First, Dad's company got caught up in a lengthy strike lockout situation. Second, there were complications concerning child-custody from a previous marriage. Third, extended family members were constantly on hand to offer advice (both positive and negative). Fourth, old health complication were rearing their head as Mom galloped from one part-time job to the next.

When breakdowns like this occur, those closest usually get the full fury of the anger, fear, and frustration. Mom's reaction was to distance herself completely from husband and kids. When she did this, Ashley's younger brother hunkered down, and let things pass over him. After all, he had grandparents, aunts, uncles and cousins who cared for him when Dad wasn't around.

But Ashley was older, more sensitive, more responsible. She realized something was radically wrong. Furthermore, because of that automatic "conspiracy of silence" that enshrouds most debilitating mental situations, Ashley kept everything to herself. She stoically carried on ... However, there was a sadness that pervaded her whole being. The sadness was there when dad loaded kids and baggage in the car, and headed off on a twelve-hour car trip to spend Christmas with his own family in B.C. It was still there when they pulled back into town four days later.

My heart ached for Ashley. She had to talk. She had to find release. I have always made a point of being "A Friend" to the children of this family, and if Ashley ever needed a friend, it was now. I invited her to lunch. We tried to chat about this and that, though I'm sure Ashley knew I had an agenda ... But each time we would approach the subject of how she felt, the pain was too deep, and she would push our conversation in a safer direction.

Somewhere along the line we made a breakthrough. "Know what I wish?" she asked. "I wish I could send my mom some flowers." She sighed the saddest sigh I've ever heard. "She's sick you know ... That's why she couldn't be with us for Christmas ... There we were together, my dad and my brother and me - and she was all alone."

The lump in my throat was as big as the tear in my eye. "I just wish I could send flowers. She would like that."

"I have a suggestion," I offered. "It is so hard to send real flowers any distance when it's this cold. But I bet she would understand if we could make up an arrangement of artificial flowers. Those could go through the mail OK. I could get her address and you could wrap the parcel. Think about the note you want to include, and I'll help you write it down."

We spent the next two hours choosing some of the remains from my Christmas decorations, boxing them, wrapping them, and enclosing a letter that read:

"Mommy I love you. I hope you get better soon."
Love, Ashley

As we took the parcel to the mail, I noticed a bit of bounce in her step, and just the trace of a lilt in her voice. As for me, I felt so privileged to have witnessed this moment of graciousness shown through the generosity of a caring five-year old.

A Family Affair

The Patriarch Isaac was forty years old when he married Rebecca.
Because Rebecca had no children for some period of time, Isaac
prayed for her, and the Lord answered his prayer. Rebecca became
pregnant. She carried twins. Even before they were born, they
struggled against each other in her womb. She said "Why should
something like this happen to me?", so she asked the Lord for an
answer. The Lord said to her "two nations are within you. You will
give birth to two rival peoples. One will be stronger than the other.
The older will serve the younger." (Genesis 25:19-24)

The Hebrews of Old were realists. Tribal families live
in close contact with each other. Tribal families are as
aware of their neighbors' good points and bad points as
are prairie folk who have lived side-by-side for many
generations. And when these Hebrew people told the stories of their patriarchs and matriarchs, they dared not
make them appear other than they actually were.

Take Isaac and Rebecca and Jacob and Esau, for
instance. It is true that, at the beginning, the story tellers
dwelt on Rebecca's beauty, and Isaac's need for an
appropriate wife. It is true that they talked about how
much the couple wanted to have a family, and what a gift
of God it was to discover that Rebecca was pregnant and
carrying twins!

But when these Hebrew people gathered around their
campfires and started telling intimate stories about family life, these stories told of life in the raw. The twin
boys were Esau and Jacob, born in that order. Not one
minute of Rebecca's pregnancy had been easy, for the
two seemed to struggle against each other from the
moment of conception. Esau was the activist, the out-
doors man, skillful in the way of the field. Jacob

appeared to be quieter and more contemplative. But we are soon to see his calculating shrewdness at work. Matter-of-fact, Dr. John Hardy, Old Testament Professor at Pine Hill Seminary, sums up Jacob's character by saying, "He was so crooked, he could hide behind a spiral staircase!" Isaac favoured Esau, and Rebecca favoured Jacob.

Family skeletons came out of the closet as the story tellers related how Rebecca helped Jacob win status in the family. They told of the family fights that went on between the brothers. They told of how Rebecca helped Jacob plot to trick Isaac and steal Esau's birthright. They told of Isaac's uncontrollable anger when he learned Jacob had fleeced him. They told of how, yet again, Rebecca stepped in to help her favoured son escape from home, hopeful that he would be delivered from the fury caused by this dastardliness.

This is not a "Little House On The Prairie" drama. This is more of the caliber of "Dallas." We begin to wonder why it even is in Scripture. We begin to wonder how the Children of Israel could ever pay tribute to patriarchs and matriarchs who had as many imperfections as did Isaac and Rebecca, and Jacob and Esau.

Our tendency, in our own families, is to try to pass over the "black sheep" as quickly as we can. Our tendency is to respond with a "thundering silence" when it comes to the rascals and villains who are our blood relations. Our tendency is to speak in hushed tones about the children who have disappointed us. Our tendency is to change the subject when someone tells us some of the more "colourful" stories about our parents or grandparents.

How, then, dare we acknowledge that Rebecca became a domineering mistress of intrigue? And that Jacob was a trickster? Maybe it is that we still have a good deal of Puritan blood in our veins, and thus feel we have been given the right to pass judgment and live in judgment over others?

This is not so for the Hebrew story tellers, for they had more important messages to communicate. The Hebrew story tellers simply told stories of how it was with the people. Their listeners knew no one was perfect. They knew families regularly have their darker moments. They accepted the people for who they were ... But looked beyond the human frailties to learn the truths of God.

From the stories of this family, they could learn much.

First, they learned how this family prayed to Yahweh, the one God above all gods. They did this in a time when many other families were tempted to add insurance coverage by dallying with the fertility gods, and the Baal gods.

Second, they were reminded that this family, too, was tempted by very human temptations, and often gave in to those temptations. However, at other times they could rise above their temptations with the help of a loving God.

Third, they were taught to accept the fact that no one is perfect. Yet God can use even imperfection to accomplish more godly things.

From this one family's story, we learn many lessons that are helpful for us even in these times.

Prayer
Lord, as we read the story of these earliest ancestors, help us rise above judgment and indignation to hear the real

story of their faith, and of their struggle to walk with you in
faithful ways.
Their journey was filled with trials and temptation,
as our journey is filled with trials and temptation.
But always, they were drawn by your love,
and directed to live faith-filled lives.
Walk with us in our journey.
Help us accept our pain ... and see beyond it. Amen.

Gus, The Barber

Clergy folks have a unique perspective on life in a small community.
At the time of death, we are drawn into the intimate lives of people
who are feeling very vulnerable. In the days and weeks and months
that follow a time of bereavement, we have opportunity to hear the
stories of grief told and retold. Ever so carefully, we also listen for
opportunities for healing. Darrel's mum was the person who told
me about her son's ongoing grief ... and of the one person who
helped him talk things through.

Darrel was six years old when his dad died. The family had just moved to the city so the lad could go to
school. The farm was forty miles away. His dad, thirty
one years old, stayed back on the farm to help with the
harvest. In spite of his arthritis and heart condition, there
was a lot the young father could do to help in this busiest
of all the seasons.

Adult members of the family had known for a long time
that Garry could probably never live to be a grandfather.
But Darrel didn't know that. In his limited experience, the
only thing he knew was that he hadn't been on the farm the
past four days, because he had to be at school. It was the
first time he hadn't been there - riding the combine, pre-
tending to drive the truck, and eating meals in the field

with the guys. Now, his dad wasn't going to be around any more. Now, his life was interrupted forever.

That's a lot for a little guy to take. That's a lot for anyone to face. He was brave, oh so brave ... for the sake of his mom ... and for the sake of his little sister. In the tradition of his family, he was "the man" now.

Others worried about this show of bravery. Grandma, who was a best friend, couldn't get him to talk. Uncle, who shared a lot of tractor time with him, couldn't get him to talk. The teacher, who tried to do all the classroom things that would be supportive of a bereaving youngster, couldn't get him to talk. It was obvious his heart was crushed. It was equally obvious he lived by the code "cowboys don't cry."

Five weeks later, Darrel needed a haircut. His mom automatically took him to Gus, the family barber. Gus pulled out the booster board, got him seated at the right height, took the comb in one hand and the scissors in the other, and began to chat. "How's it going?" It seemed like such a simple question. But for Darrel, that was the key that opened his heart. Always before, he had come with his dad to this place, to this person, to have his hair cut. Gus and his dad and he shared something special. He knew that Gus would understand. He told Gus everything that happened. He talked with Gus about how he interpreted his situation now that he was "the man of the family." He confessed to Gus that he really missed his dad a lot!

Gus had that special sensitivity that barbers often have. He recognized the importance of the moment, and of the story shared. He took extra time with the cut, to make sure the boy could finish saying what lay deep in his heart. They affirmed that both of them felt the loss. They affirmed that it was important for Darrel to get on with his schooling. They affirmed that any time either of them needed to talk, they could get together.

With that, Darrel thanked Gus, shook hands, gave a brave smile of appreciation, and set off to face the world again. Obviously he had left more than a few clippings of hair there on the floor of Gus's Barber Shop.

Thanks be to God for caring people as sensitive as this man!

Two Solitudes

Many rural Canadians live near Aboriginal Communities. But too few have friends there.

"That's a police ghost car!" the hitchhiker in my car commented as a pale blue Chev passed us. The woman was from the Blackfoot Reserve at Gleichen, and was on her way to Calgary to take care of some important family business. It was blistering hot, and she and her traveling companion had been standing on the roadside for four hours trying to get a ride to the city. They had come in to the United Church at Strathmore earlier that afternoon to get out of the sun, and to get a cold drink ... That is when I had first talked to them ... That is why I was surprised to see the woman still on the highway two hours later, exhausted and dehydrated.

"Could you wait for my cousin?" she asked when I stopped for her. "He always stands down the road a bit so he can identify the car I get in, in case some guy tries to take advantage of me."

That was a first reminder of just how different the worlds are that we live in: I, a non-native clergy person; and she, a native from the Blackfoot Reserve.

I could hardly believe they had been standing in the

heat all those hours. But she explained that the family matter was urgent, and they had to get to Calgary today. The problem was that there were no other natives on the highway that day because they were all getting ready to move in for the Stampede the next day.

Fortunately, I had an over large bottle of cold Sprite that I was taking as part of my contribution to the potluck supper in the city. It was as I was sharing this with them that she noticed the passing vehicle, and drew my attention to it. "That's a police ghost car," was her comment. Then, surprised that I had no reaction, she looked directly at me and said, "It doesn't really matter to you, does it?"

"No, come to think of it, it doesn't." My car had cruise-control, and we were going slower than usual because the man in the back seat was pouring pop into styrofoam cups. "No, it doesn't matter to me," I agreed. "But obviously it does to you."

"There are four ghost cars along here. We know every one of them," she said. "They stop us quite regularly." That was another reminder of just how different the worlds were that we lived in: I, a non-native clergy person; and she a native from The Reserve.

What had started out to be a simple drive into the city on a boiling hot summer afternoon, in the air conditioned comfort of my car, suddenly turned into an occasion that set my mind spinning in a thousand directions.

There we lived, side-by-side ... two worlds ... two solitudes ... But mine was the controlling solitude because I was white! I wondered just how many other differences there were? Differences that I am not even aware of because I am white! ... Because, by some accident of nature, I am a member of the part of society that writes the rules, and enforces the laws.

The Story of Daniel

(A condensed version written by Church Board members)

The Church Board took time out from business matters to do a Bible Study. I challenged them to choose a subject, spend time discussing it, then suggest to me how this subject might be presented in the context of a worship service. Part of the group gave leadership at the actual service, some of the others wrote a Readers' Digest version of the story so we could print it in the Bulletin.

Daniel and his three friends were captured and taken as slaves to a far away country. Because they were well-trained, intelligent, strong young men, they were brought before the King of that country.

First it was ordered that their Hebrew names be changed to Babylonian names. Daniel became Belteshazzar, Hananiah was called Shadrach, Mishael was named Meshach, and Azariah was called Abednego.

Second, they were ordered to eat the food and wine provided for them, in spite of their own religious laws about food.

Two incidents are particularly outstanding in the lives of these young men. Their captor, King Nebucadnessar, the Babylonian King, had a great statue made. It was ninety feet tall and covered with gold. He ordered that all his subjects, when they heard a certain musical sound, should bow down and worship that idol. Naturally Daniel and his friends refused, for they worshiped only one God. Because of their disobedience, they were thrown in the midst of a huge fire ... But their own God protected them, and they were not burned.

Then the Persians captured King Nebucadnessar, and the city, and the royal palace, and Daniel and his friends also. The new King, King Darius, soon made friends with the young Jews. That friendship made the courtiers jealous, so they tricked the king into passing a law making it illegal to ask anything of any god or any person except the king (for thirty days). Those who disobeyed were to be cast into a den of lions. Then the jealous courtiers waited, and watched. They knew Daniel prayed to his God three times a day.

Of course it wasn't long before the jealous courtiers reported Daniel's activities to King Darius. There was nothing the King could do but enforce his own law. But "surely your God will save you," the king suggested as he accompanied Daniel to the lion's den. And it was true. Early the next morning, when the king saw that the lions had not hurt Daniel, he ordered Daniel's release, and brought him back to the court as a friend and advisor. He also commanded that "everyone should fear and respect Daniel's God."

A Few Thoughts We Shared In Our Meditation

Daniel and his friends had no easy time of it. This is a document about how three young people suffered because of racial discrimination. They were ordered to change their names, for the Babylonians believed Babylonian names were better than Jewish names. They were forced to eat strange foods that were forbidden according to their religious customs. And they were forced to deny their religious heritage and bow before a statue of the Babylonian King.

The Babylonians had no respect for the Jewish people, but instead tried to show their superiority over them. Still in the end, the story tells us, God stood alongside the young men and helped them face their ordeal ....

We talked a bit about some of the ways racism colours our own world. For example, we see a couple of Native people on the street who have been injured because of alcohol and drug abuse, and we shake our heads in disgust. A little further on, we see a couple of thirty-five year old lads with white skins. They too suffer from drug burnout. We shake our heads in sorrow. "Poor David!" we say. Or "My heart goes out to Jim's mother. It must be such a burden!"

People in our town often comment, too, about the ambulance from The Reserve always being seen in town. Between the lines is the suggestion that someone is certainly abusing the system. These insinuations come so easily, and few people call us to task. Would it be any different if we lived twenty miles away from the hospital and only a few of our friends had vehicles? How many times might we call the local ambulance then? And even now, so many of our seniors and handicapped would be sadly neglected if it weren't for the generous "Care Bear" transporting services provided through the local Lions' Club.

Without trying to be offensive or intrusive, we simply tried to name some of the issues that touched our own lives. The discussion humbled all of us.

In closing, we acknowledge how, through studying this scripture story and discussing the Gospel message, we were reminded that prejudice and racism are not appropriate for those who believe themselves to be part of the Family of God.

Prayer

You who come to us as Parent and Friend, help us to see ourselves in the broader context of your world. Help us act with wisdom as we understand more about Your care and Your intent. Amen.

Julia - A Memoir

written by Diane Burt Stuckey

*Oft time we work so hard at focusing on the positive that we over-
look another person's grief. As people have talked with the Stuckey
family over the years, they talk about the one child who lived, but
seldom speak of the two children who died. I shall always be grateful to Diane for sharing this deeply felt story with me. We talked
about these things as we prepared for the baptism of number two
daughter.*

Julia was the first born of premature triplets on
September 15, 1987 at the Lethbridge Regional Hospital.
To my amazement, she cried when she was born.
Weighing hardly more than a pound of butter, she was
perfect in every way.

Our triplets were starting their 24th week of gestation.
Their odds of survival were slim we were told, but at
least they were born alive. Baby C, Daniel, was taken
into God's hands shortly after birth - at 320 grams he
was too small to survive. Baby A, Julia, and Baby B,
Joshua, were stabilized and then transported by heli-
copter to the Foothills Hospital in Calgary early that
evening.

Julia was a very sick littler girl right from the beginning ... she endured one medical crisis after another, it
seemed. She had her good days, and her bad weeks.
Although her weight gain and determination to live kept
us optimistic, her bad lungs and dependency on the ven-
tilator kept us realistic. It was like living on the edge
from hour to hour. We were so grateful for each day she
lived, yet our prayers were for that "something" that
would turn things around and tip the scales in her favor.
It was a miracle that she had come this far - couldn't we

be granted one more? It was not to be.

As her struggle for oxygen became more and more difficult, our hopes began to fade. We agonized over the decision we faced. Selfishly, we could not possibly let our sweet little girl go. But in our hearts, how could we continue to keep her alive? We knew that further medical intervention would only prolong her struggle, and that time could offer no hope for improvement or quality of life. Once again we asked God to reach out ... this time to take our precious baby girl.

The night of February 27th, 1988, was a special time with Julia, shared by people that loved her and had cared for her. After disconnecting her from life support, we took turns holding her and cuddling her. Our tears fell and our hearts ached with grief. But we could see that the pain was gone from her face, and her body no longer racked by machine to give her breath. We could hold her with no tubes, wires, IV's, or struggle. She looked so peaceful and so beautiful. We knew we had made the right decision.

Julia has been gone for almost three months now (as I make these notes). But she LIVED 165 days! We have many wonderful memories of our time with her, and we feel blessed to have known her personality and her sense of being. The living serve to teach us so much about life, death, courage, hope, prayer, joy, grief, sorrow - a lifetime of learning in only a few short months. Her life touched the hearts of many, in the hospital and in the community. This is truly a tribute to a little girl who never left the Intensive Care Unit.

It is now five years later that I have the courage to type this story, and I still think of her daily and feel the pain of her loss deeply. The gift of Joshua serves to remind us of the two babies that we lost - as he goes off to kindergarten each day, I still think "what if ...?"

The prayer that hung above Julia in her hospital crib helped me to keep things in perspective then, and has helped me to move forward despite our trials and losses.

God grant me the Serenity
to accept the things I cannot change;
Courage to change the things I can;
and Wisdom to know the difference.

Julia, we will always love you. Even though you have a little sister now, you will always be our first born, precious little girl. Nothing, not even time, can take that away from us.

New Generations Seek Old Truths

Church folk are often driven by guilt. In addition to very busy lives, they feel a deep responsibility for maintaining the institutional church. One group of young people opted to try something different. I applaud their efforts, and encourage them to celebrate and share their vision. The Spirit works in exciting and surprising ways in each generation.

A friend of mine from a nearby community told me that she, her husband, and three other young couples were "taking a sabbatical from the Church." But by the intensity of her questions thus far in the conversation, I was sure that spiritual matters were uppermost in her thinking. "We feel we need some nurture," she said, "and there are those in the church who just want us to keep busy ... So we've opted to form a group of our own."

79

I knew all the participants she had mentioned. Each had young children, worked hard in their various vocations, and contributed to the church and community in a variety of ways. "We need to add depth to our lives. But we seem to spend most of our church time teaching Sunday School, helping with fund-raisers, and defending ourselves because we don't sing in the choir."

These four couples and their families enjoyed being together. It happened at a social gathering one evening that one of the women shared her excitement over a new book she had been reading. They talked about the book into the evening, and that was when they decided to get together at a regular time to discuss other spiritual matters. Problem was, the only regular time they had was Sunday morning, when they would otherwise be in church.

"It's not that we have anything against our new minister. She's great! But we need space to talk with each other."

"Sounds like a great idea," I reflected. "But stop flailing yourself over not going to church. Tell you minister what you are doing, and why. Put a memo in the Sunday bulletin so everyone knows. You aren't dropping out. You are just trying something a little different. Maybe there are others who think like you do."

"You really think it's OK?" She bubbled with enthusiasm. "We aren't stepping out of line?"

"You are right on track with others your age. Some would call you 'The Baby Boomerang Generation." Did you know that? According to the journal article I just read, everything you've told me suggests you aren't alone in how you feel, or what you are trying to do."

Her eyes glistened with tears of relief. "You mean we're normal? Baby Boomerang eh!" She giggled.

"That's interesting ... Come to think of it, we have our
own name for the old guard who were bugging us. We
call them 'The Doilies'!"

We both had a good laugh as we turned back into our
busy worlds. "God bless."

Scripture Reading   Isaiah 11: 1 - 10

*(This was probably written during the seventh century before the
Christian Era, and some wonder if this might have been a prophecy
referring to the coming of Christ as the Messiah.)*

The royal line of David is like a tree that has been cut down;
but just as new branches sprout from a stump,
so a new king will arise from among David's descendants.
The spirit of the Lord will give him wisdom
and the knowledge and skill to rule his people.
He will know the Lord's will and will have reverence for him,
and find pleasure in obeying him.
He will not judge by appearance or hearsay;
he will judge the poor fairly and defend the rights of the
helpless...
He will rule his people with justice and integrity ...
The land will be as full of the knowledge of the Lord
as the seas are full of water.

Musings

Does the Institutional Church really care about the
unique needs of the Baby Boomerang Generation?
Congregations may be frustrated when these younger
people aren't in the pews in large numbers.
Congregational members may chide them for not carrying their part of the burden. But I don't often hear these

same church folks invite this large portion of the population to contribute to the life of the Faith Community in their own unique way!

I believe the Boomerangers have a great need for many of the things the Church has to offer. However, they want to seek after their spirituality in their own way. They recognize their need to "grow a soul," to learn how to meditate, to find a moral framework that can be a base for their lives. Because everything about them is in a constant state of flux and change, they recognize their need, also, to continually re-evaluate their spirituality. Rituals are more important than ever, yet even these are re-applied as reality and circumstance demand.

The crucial thing for the Baby Boomerang Generation is learning how to assume responsibility for themselves, and learning how to handle the variety of crises that continually touch their lives and the lives of those they love.

Will "The Doilies" be there, to walk with them along the way? It could be a very rich and rewarding encounter.

Brokenness and Healing

The story of a man who was sick for 38 years is found in John 5: 1-18

When I read this Biblical story, the first word that comes to mind is FEAR. FEAR controlled this man's life, and FEAR was his greatest handicap.

Imagine yourself visiting ancient Jerusalem. Imagine yourself approaching the Temple area. There is a pool there that bubbles up from time to time, probably because of the springs that feed it. Some believe this bubbling to be the work of the angels ... Legends have spread suggesting that the pool has mystical power for anyone who can get into the water while there is still some turbulence. Those who gather daily at the edge of the pool include the blind, the lame, and the paralyzed. Today our attention is drawn to one who has, in fact, been visiting this place for 38 years ... but has yet to be healed. As a matter-of-fact, he has yet to get himself into the water at the appropriate time!

Jesus, visiting in the city, approaches the gathering at the pool, watches the action of the water, and the people crowded there. His attention is particularly drawn to this one person. But it doesn't take long for a stranger to notice how different this man is from the others. His condition appears to be chronic. His case is pitiable. There is little about him that is attractive ... There is much to suggest that his infirmity might even be used as an excuse!

Jesus approaches the man, understanding why it is possible that no one has succeeded in helping him get to the water. It is because the man bristles with hostility and anger. "Do you want to be healed?" Jesus asks. The man's excuses are many. He blames others for his plight. "Nobody will help me. While I'm trying to get to the water, other so-and-so's barge in ahead of me!"

Jesus can sense the fear that has made this man close in on himself. The man hates with vindictive bitterness. The man finds comfort only when he can lash out at others. His grungy, dirty sleeping mat is his place of refuge from the realities of the world. "Come now," Jesus challenges without even attempting to bring him near the water. "Come on. Get up. Pick up your mat and walk." "And immediately," Scripture tells us, "the man got up, picked up his mat ... and walked."

Yet even this "healing miracle" had little real effect on

the man. Now he blamed the interfering stranger for taking his excuse away! Now that he could walk, he was sure more would be expected of him ... and that was a threat! His legs might have been healed, but his spirit was more in bondage than ever.

Next, we have the scene on the street! The man is lumbering down the roadway, mumbling to himself about all the knocks he has had in life. A couple of Orthodox Jews meet him ... and accuse him of breaking the Laws of the Sabbath. Most certainly, they believe no one is allowed to work on the Sabbath ... not even so much as to carry a bedmat. The man became enraged when they challenged him. He grew vindictive as he retold his story.

"Who made you carry this burden?" the holy ones asked, rubbing their hands. But the man didn't know. Fear and panic had so blinded him, he never bothered to notice who the man was.

Finally, we have the scene in the Temple. Jesus sees the man from the Temple steps, and approaches to advise him. He says, "You really are well now. Just stop this wailing and wrangling ... or something worse may happen to you. Far from taunting the man, Jesus was acting out of compassion. He recognized the man would never be better till he could find peace with himself! He was suggesting there was a worse bondage then being hopelessly tied to a mat by a healing pool for thirty eight years! He was trying to point out the possibilities this man had to experience freedom and love, and thereby conquer his FEAR.

Each of us have his or her own bondage of fear that cripples us and excludes us from so many good things in life! There is fear in each of us. But it is always so much easier to recognize the fear in someone else, while we hold tight to our own crutches ... and our own excuses.

Many elderly fear because of failing health. They curse their ears, that don't hear so well ... and their hands, that are clumsy ... and their feet that hurt all the time ...!

Many young fear because they can't get jobs ... can't pay their bills ... They curse the government ... their parents ... the whole darn world ...!

The middle aged fear because they feel stressed and stretched to the limit ... They have no time ... They have lost the power to sort out priorities ... and to appreciate the gift of each moment.

Maybe John tells the story of the man handicapped by fear to make us think ... to help us hear the futility of our excuses ... to remind us to look upward and outward ... to trust that if we let go of our crutch, even for a moment, good things can happen.

This story also helps us think about how we can have more patience with each other. When people we know use all their old excuses, we so easily ignore them ... or become angry with them. Yet Jesus saw the potential in this stranger, and took time to reach out to him in spite of the barbs and nettles. Jesus recognized an opportunity for healing. Healing the body was the man's responsibility. But Jesus believed this man's soul, also, could be made whole. He set the scene so this one person could become free to be himself!

If ever that man could get over his own hang-ups, I'm sure he would have so much to offer. He had witnessed so much pain in those 38 years by the pool. He had seen so many miracles. There would be a depth of wisdom in that experience. A compassionate heart in one like this could offer support and encouragement to even the most hopeless and helpless. A loving heart, in the midst of so many who were filled with despair, could point to new horizons.

Prayer

Ever compassionate God, help us to see ourselves as others see us. Help us to let loose of our crutches, our hang-ups, our excuses ... that we may discover the wonderful potential you have given us. Free our arms and our hearts, that we might reach out in love. Amen

"Strength does not mean the absence of suffering ...
... It means something else ...
    - letting the tears flow when the pain comes
    - letting the tears cleanse the spirit
the way a summer shower freshens the air.
Without vulnerability, I cannot love ...
And without love, I cannot struggle ...
Without struggle, there is no growth ...
    ... there is only death!"

Shirley Endicotte

Grandfather's Open Arms
written by Erin Phillips

Erin Phillips, chaplain with the Ecumenical Campus Ministry in Lethbridge, Alberta, wrote this thoughtful meditation for the local newspaper.

Not long ago I visited my grandmother who has lived in the same house since before I was born. Over the years changes have been made to the upstairs, but the basement remains the same.

When I was a child, the basement was a place of great adventure and mystery. Its walls were lined with shelves upon which sat every kind of object. Boxes, tools, suitcases, household appliances, unidentified objects, all waited there to spark the imagination. The cat, an elderly, long-haired creature, took refuge from the attentions of noisy, rough, inquisitive children, high and out-of-reach among the paint cans. Gone now, but present years ago, was a big stuffed chair which could be a ship or a cave, depending on the game.

This all came back to me on the last morning of my visit as I descended the same worn wooden stairs. I vividly remembered the day when I was four or five, and I went exploring aboard the good ship Stuffed Chair, oblivious to the activity above me. It was the day I first learned the meaning of forgiveness.

I was lost in my game when my mother called me from the top of the stairs. "I'm here," I called out and returned to my game. I did not bother to check to see what she wanted. If I had, I would have discovered that she hadn't heard me.

Happily I played on while above me the family grew increasingly alarmed. As they searched the property - the ditch at the side of the road, the water's edge - I played on. When I finally ascended the stairs, their relief at seeing me alive and well quickly turned to anger that I had so thoughtlessly frightened them.

After the family assembled in the living room, I found myself the unhappy centre of attention. My mother told me to apologize to my grandfather for scaring him so badly. I was, by this point, regretting that I had come up the stairs and would have happily disappeared from view. I looked over at my grandfather anticipating his anger. He looked at me, smiled gently and opened his arms. I disappeared then into his embrace.

Years later as a teenager I would read the story in Luke's Gospel of the son who takes his inheritance and goes off to squander it. He leaves a father behind who no doubt worries about him. He runs into trouble and out of money. Desperate, he returns to his father fearful of the reception he will find. Instead of being angry and rejecting his son, however, we read that, "while the son was still far off, his father saw him and was filled with compassion; he ran and put his arms around him and kissed him (Luke 15:20)."

Jesus tells this story to communicate to his followers the depth and breadth of God's forgiveness and compassion towards us. This was a lesson I learned first from my grandfather. His open arms became for me the first taste of what I would later experience as the Good News of Jesus Christ.

For this is the good news that we receive and we proclaim. That while we were still far off, God saw us and was filled with compassion. He ran up to us, put his arms around and kissed us. And we who are lost, who have failed our families, who have screwed up, are able to disappear into his embrace.

Expressions of Faith

DON BRESTLER '84

   Most of the early settlers on the prairies faced loneliness and hardship and poverty. They were short on cash, and had little by way of security. But they did have each other learned to survive a lot of tough times by working together.

   That prairie spirit continues to this day. It is evident in the way those that live here care for each other, and in the way they learn to accept their limitations. They make the best of it.

   These are not always a church going people, but they are profoundly aware of the Spirit of God in their midst. They learn to hear "The Word of The Lord" as they moved through life; as they move through their everyday activities.

   Sometimes their God is there as a source of explanation for what otherwise is unknown. Sometimes their God is the one with whom they can have a "damn good argument"!

Tribute To Darryl Vance

written by Linda Austen

A word of recognition and a belt buckle given by one's peers at the Cowboy Poetry Gathering ... What finer way is there to say thank you!

We live now in the nineties, but our longings do persist
For the kind of men our friend is;
So few of them exist.

He walks in strength and honor. They are traits that
mark this man.
He rides the horse called freedom
With the people of the land.
He's rugged like the mountains. He stands for what is right.
He honors God and country.
Monumental is his height.

Grassy Butte, the family homestead, still stands and
not by chance,
Its honor and tradition
Carried on by Darryl Vance.
Blue Canadian Rockies, rolling hills and stretching land:
Their size and strength are needed
To match this kind of man.

Independent rancher ... Cowboy through and through ...
Integrity and honesty ...
His neighbors call him true.
His love for wife and family, protects them and defends.
That love then grows ... expanding
Encompassing his friends.
They still exist ... these heroes, humanity at its best,
Becoming living legends
Of the Great Canadian West.

Pushing Back The Darkness

In Genesis we find three interesting statements about "Darkness" and "Light". When life gets chaotic, and our lives are threatened by the forces of darkness, it helps to hold on to these images. "In the beginning God ..." God was there first. Even before there was anything else, God was there!

. "The earth was without form ... and darkness was upon the face of the deep ..." There was nothing except this huge, seething, black, chaotic darkness.

. "And God said 'Let there be light;' and there was light, and God saw that it was good!" The very first thing that God wanted to do, and was able to do, was create light. This was the basis from which everything else grew ... "And God saw that it was good!"

I find this imagery of light and darkness to be very helpful, for I have been in those situations where darkness bred its own kind of fear. And the blackness of the situation seemed to hold me in its grip.

Above all, I remember what a difference the light made. Sometimes it was only a pinprick of light .... Sometimes it was as distant as the starlit sky .... But once the light came into focus, the terror of the darkness seemed to melt away.

In the Gospel of John (1:4-5), the writer connects the earliest times with the times of Jesus. Before the time of Creation, "The Word" was already there ... and "That Word was life, and the life was the light of all.... The Light shines in the darkness, and the darkness has not overcome it." For so many years, that "light" was centered in Jesus Christ, "The Word became flesh!" The story of the crucifixion tells about the brightness of the Light being threatened. "Darkness fell over all the land"

(Matthew 25:45) as the powers of chaos again threatened to engulf the earth. But ultimately the chaotic powers of death were pushed aside. The Resurrection Story talks about the appearance of the angel at the tomb ... whose appearance was so brilliant it was "like lightening". The raiment of this messenger "shone white as snow." (Matthew 28:3)

Can you sense the constant struggle in this imagery? The chaotic powers of darkness are always there, festering like a cancerous growth, ready to consume whatever they touch. These are the harbingers of fear, and pain, and despair. But the Light seems always to be within reach, at the ready to flood out the darkness ... and bring its own soothing message of peace and hope.

Remember how it was during the Calgary Olympics? The lighting of the torch on Mt. Olympus seemed so manufactured, so "made for TV." Even when the runners started to carry the light across the country, many doubted the spectacle. They scoffed at how this could have any possible significance.

But the torch moved across the land. Cauldrons were lit in each city. Candles were carried to many homes. The light spread ... and with it, the expectation grew that maybe we could "pull it off!" The Olympics were being held right here, on our own doorstep! And they were going to be the best darned Games ever!

I don't have to tell you about how the light spread, and with it the spirit of hope and enthusiasm. The greatest memory, for me, was the closing event ... held at night. At the opening ceremonies, we could see the crowds. We could watch the spectacle fill the entire stadium. But at the closing ceremonies, the crowds were gobbled up in the darkness. We could see only what the spotlights chose to show us.

Each person in the stadium had been given a torch candle, to be lighted at the end of the ceremony. But, as the athletes streamed into the stadium, they shared their lights with the audience. One candle was used to light another ... and another ... until there were thousands of little red lights sparkling across the field ... and in the end zones ... and in tiers behind us! Immediately the mood changed. No longer was there that feeling of hollow emptiness. Now there was a warmth, a sense of pride, a sense of togetherness, a sense of hope.

Eventually the official cauldron was extinguished. But we had the sense that we were carrying bits of that light with us, beyond the darkness of the stadium, and into the rest of our lives. It was truly a great moment.

Each Sunday, as we light the Christ candle, the prayer is that the same kind of experience can happen among those who gather for worship. We can experience the light of God's presence. We can take the glow of that light into our everyday lives, and our everyday world. We can share in bringing a new dawn to even one tiny corner where the powers of chaos once ruled. This is our privilege. This is why faithful ones are often called "The Children of the Light."

Stained Glass Windows

Mrs. Kenneth Hamilton (University of Winnipeg) was doing some research on a Red River Oxcart-Train of stained glass windows that were being transported from Ontario to St. Boniface Cathedral in Winnipeg. I started to laugh when I heard this, for I could only imagine the profanities muttered by a wagon-master who had to deliver such a load.

But Mrs. Hamilton patiently corrected my ribald outburst when she reminded me just how important these windows were for the sanity of frontier people - especially the women. The cathedrals and churches of that era were the centres of art, culture, and civilization. They represented a semblance of order and hope for settlers who had left everything behind to settle this uncouth and unknown land!

These are facts we so often forget today when we have art galleries, music halls, and media of all sorts at the tips of our fingers. Mrs. Hamilton instilled in me a new respect for old churches, and for special sacred places.

Exclusive Dinner Ware
Tells Its Own Stories

One of the most treasured possessions of many older prairie women is their Wedgwood China. This touch of refinement has helped them see beyond the hard work and harsh conditions they often had to face. Look at the story behind the story, and those pieces of porcelain mean even more.

Imagine yourself and your family living in England in the early Seventeen Hundreds. It is well before Wolfe and Montcalm went to battle on the Plains of Abraham in Lower Canada. Conditions were desperate for all but the wealthiest of English families. They lived in dark, dirty, thatched houses that crawled with insects and vermin. They were rough, uncouth people who drank heavily and died before they got old. What little food they could scrape together was served out of the same container in which it was cooked. Everyone sopped their food from the central "trencher" (or bowl) in the middle of the table. Thus, they exchanged disease and contamination every time they ate!

Against this background, I invite you to focus your attention on the Wedgwood Family - who had been serving as "Potters" in England for 400 years. Though we think today of Wedgwood China being something that is very elegant, very costly, and most exclusive, this was not the case when Josiah Wedgwood was a young boy. They were a family with a trade, but with nothing in the way of status or income. They were crafts people. Most definitely they were not gentry. They lived in conditions that were particularly appalling because they had to be immediately adjacent to the clay and fuel that was so necessary to their trade.

Josiah Wedgwood is the person who commands our special attention. He was born in 1730, the youngest of thirteen children. He was not healthy from the start. His father died when he was nine years old, so he was taken from school and put to work in the pottery. When he was eleven years old, he contracted smallpox. He recovered from the disease, but his right leg was affected, and he was left permanently lame. Eventually, that leg was amputated below the knee.

Josiah Wedgwood's older brother was supposed to teach him the pottery business. But because of his lame leg, it was soon obvious to the brother (who didn't want to bother with this sickly under-aged bit of humanity) that there was no place for him in the business.

But Josiah Wedgwood was one of those individuals who saw adversity to be a blessing in disguise. He never gave up the pottery business, though he had to continue by finding a partner who would help him start his own business.

True, his handicap prevented his sitting at the wheel for any length of time. So this lad focused his attention on research and experimentation. His efforts in this regard revolutionized both the pottery trade, and the entire industrial age.

He developed a ware that could be thrown on the wheel, or cast with equal facility. His experimenting led to the discovery of a rich, creamy coloured earthenware ... and eventually to the white, blue and green jasper that we associate with Wedgwood china today.

The porcelain containers he made could resist strong acids and corrosives, and thus were a boon for apothecaries and chemists. Also, he invented the Pyrometer, a thermometer to measure the highest degrees of heat.

The business grew. And at the head of the business was an industrialist with a heart! Because of his own upbringing, and because of his own disability, Josiah Wedgwood was especially sensitive to the poverty and heartbreak the average person in his community faced. Furthermore, he resolved to do something about it. As the business grew, he did what he could to build a decent town. He was a good employer who was liberal with those who worked for him. He maintained good working conditions, and paid good wages. He patiently trained the local folk to become skilled crafts people, though this often meant working with them while they were still hung-over from spending the previous night in the ale houses.

When mud and mire made it impossible for him to get his product to market, he set his mind to design engineering - and worked to build canals and waterways that changed England's transportation system.

Wedgwood's artistic designs were appreciated at home and abroad. Queen Charlotte liked his work so much that she appointed him "Potter To Her Majesty," and his "Queen's Ware" was immediately held in high demand in England and throughout the colonies. Catherine, Empress of Russia, ordered a thousand-piece dinner service - which dinner guests stole from their hostess, plate by plate. And even though he was Potter to King George III, he came out openly in favour of the American Revolution.

Josiah Wedgwood was, above all things, a reformer. He started by making a commitment that he would try to provide a plate for every person! He wanted no more common "trencher" on the table, for he was certain many diseases were spread by people eating from a common dish. Besides, he reasoned, even the poorest men and women had the right to be treated with dignity. The staple ware had to be made cheap enough for the poor to afford them. Josiah saw to that, even though there was little profit in the business!

Also, Josiah Wedgwood sympathized with the American Colonies in their plight for freedom. To help make the cause of the freedom fighters more popular, he designed and sold medallions of George Washington and Ben Franklin.

Humour, too, became a powerful tool in Wedgwood's hand. He genuinely opposed one particular political move that William Pitt was trying to promote in Ireland, so he made ten thousand containers with the image of Pitt on the bottom. The containers were spittoons, and the motto on the side read, "We will spit on Mr. Pitt!"

Wedgwood devoted his later life to getting rid of the African slave trade, which he saw to be a terrible desecration of humanity. To do this, he designed a medallion called "The Slave In Chains" medallion. On one side was a cameo of the slave in chains. On the other side was a motto that read, "Am I not a man and a brother?" This became the seal of the "Society For The Abolition of Slavery." They used their seal in a variety of ways to popularize their cause. Not only was it used in pamphlets, but as an inlaid cameo in gold snuff boxes for the nobility and the gentry; and in bracelets, buttons and pins for the ladies. Thus, for once, fashion was seen to promote the cause of justice, humanity, and freedom! Subsequently, largely as a result of these efforts, the African slave trade was abolished.

Some may ask what Wedgwood china, and the story of Josiah Wedgwood has to do with the Gospel? In my books, this is the Gospel Story. This is how one man overcame tremendous obstacles of pain and humiliation, and social and economic stigma, while holding on to the belief that the world could be made to be a better place.

John Wesley was conducting a revival in the area where Wedgwood's factory was. There, he tipped his hat in tribute to this man by saying "(Josiah Wedgwood) was small and lame, but his soul was not far from God."

Elaine Ryan, who wrote an excellent biography of Wedgwood, says of this Master Potter, "His life made our subsequent lives easier as he demonstrated his love and concern for others. He left more than a cup and plate for everyone!" Decent living and working conditions, trained crafts people, a reasonable living wage, and a plate for each person ... these all are things we take for granted today. But reformers like Josiah Wedgwood cared enough to insist that these changes were necessary. They were mindful of the human side of the Industrial Revolution.

In 1986, as Rick Hansen's "Man In Motion" Tour* made its way around the world, the Wedgwood Company acknowledged and honoured the tradition of their "little, sickly, lame" patriarch. How much it must have meant to the Tour for this most prestigious company to issue a limited edition "Man In Motion Commemorative Plate." It was ivory design on blue jasper. It was made to "Celebrate Courage." Its inscription reads:

> *"Wedgwood celebrates the courageous efforts of Rick Hansen's 'Man In Motion' World Tour to raise awareness and funds for Spinal Cord Research and Rehabilitation."*

Think of it! Think of how once again fashion has been used "to promote the cause of justice and humanity and freedom." Think of how this exclusive dinner ware company has used its wealth and influence to promote human dignity and human endeavor.

How appropriate! The roots of this go back all the way to 18th century England ... to the little man who believed in the love of God for even the poorest of creatures ... and dared to make that dream come true.

Footnote:

* Between 1985 and 1987, at 27 years of age, with absolutely no use of his legs, Rick Hansen wheeled himself 25,000 miles around the world. He visited 34 countries, and he raised twenty-four million dollars. This money has been directed toward spinal cord research and rehabilitation.

Give to Us Laughter
by Walter Farquharson

Walter's roots are deep in the prairie sod. Not only did he grow up in rural Saskatchewan, but he and Joan have now retired in the very community where they served their entire ministry. Through his ministry, his poetry, and his wise leadership, The Very Reverend Walter Farquharson has helped The Church become more compassionate.
My special wish would be that everyone who sings this song could be touched by his deep, gentle, rolling chuckles

Give to us laughter, O source of our life.
Laughter can banish to much of our strife.
Laughter and love give us wholeness and health.
Laughter and love are the coin of true wealth.

Give to us laughter as sign of deep joy,
let us in laughing find Christian employ.
joining with stars and with bright northern lights,
laughing and praising and sharing delights.

Why do we worry that we will lose face?
Why act like king for the whole human race?
often in family, and often with friend,
laughing at pride causes anguish to end.

Even in sorrow and hours of grief,
laughter with tears bring most healing relief.
God, give us laughter, and God, give us peace,
joys of your presence among us increase.

Walk Softly In Springtime

Edna Grant, the writer of this hymn, was blind. Close your eyes and listen for the sounds that surround you.

Walk softly in springtime, to hear the grass sing
its whispering carols to Jesus our King,
to see the new flowers bright colours display,
to tell all the children of glad Easter day.

Sing gently in springtime, and join with the birds,
who warble their music, a song without words,
that floats through the air and that reaches the sky,
a message of love to the father on high.

Praise gladly in springtime when earth seems to glow
with new life and colour in all things that grow;
for all nature's children are happy to say,
Rejoice, for the Saviour is risen today.

by Edna Grant

J. CANTELON

Text: Edna Fay Grant
*Text © 1965 The Hymn Society. Used by permission of Hope Publishing
Co., Carol Stream, Il. 60188. All rights reserved*

Remembering the Saints

This meditation is based on a true life experience combined with reminders of reality found in the old Russian Folk Tale "Once There Was A Tree".

The first couple of years I lived in Pincher Creek, I did a lot of work landscaping my yard. I had to clear out what was overgrown, pull out what was dead, haul in dirt, and dig patches for garden space. Next, I found some old dead trees, and placed sections of these in strategic places in my garden patches. Only then did I begin the planting ... and the transplanting.

That was five years ago. I'm sure many people wondered if I was daft. Especially, they wondered about my searching out those old dead tree-trunks. But this spring it is absolutely amazing to look again at those garden patches, and move the old stumps that lay partially exposed. A wonderful living world exists around those old stumps ... beetles and bugs of all sorts hide under the rotting wood, and in the cracks and crevices. And birds perch on the stumps: to sing, and to have their dinner. There is a vitality in my garden, a life that gives birth to more life. Out of what others might have considered to be dead, a whole new world has emerged. Summer and winter, my garden remains as a place of refuge and life.

I like to relate this imagery to the Church. Oft times we look at our Church and shake our heads in despair. We can hardly imagine there being hope for the future ... We get locked into thinking of the church as if it were like one of those dying trees ... We remember the good times, the past times when kids hung from the branches of the tree; we laughed and enjoyed picnics under the shade; and we recognized God as the source of all that we had. But we feel sadness because that-was-then, and this-is-now! We sing a dirge naming evidence of death in the old tree ... and fear it will soon become obsolete.

We do the same with the Church. People count heads on Sunday morning, and comment that there are fewer and fewer at the service. Others start wondering, out loud, about how long they can afford a minister. Others shake their heads when it is suggested we move into an upgrading project. They are hesitant to invest too much because they prophecy that the old roots could give out completely. Hence, we hasten our own demise and toll the death knell long before the reality exists.

I am so glad I was raised on the prairies, in the Palliser Triangle area where we were surrounded by end-less rolling hills of short-grass, and sand, and shimmering horizon. While others tell me how little there is to see and do in what they call the great empty prairie, I look for other realities. I know that a prairie slough offers a whole world of wonder and discovery - because I played around these sloughs when I was a youngster. I know that sandstone rocks record messages that are hundreds of years old, and that clay cliffs erode away to reveal dinosaur bones ... As a child, I would search the windswept fields for arrowheads and evidence of ancient civilization. My eyes automatically scan the horizon for antelope and grouse. And, if I was ever bored, I needed to only roll over on my back and imagine the stories of "Ghost Riders" written in the clouds.

It isn't that this prairie world is different for me than for our casual visitors. But it is that my family and I have a different understanding about these prairie scapes because this is our home. This is the source of who we are.

That is why, today, I remain the optimist - about life,

and about the church. There is evidence that our old ways of doing things in the church are dying. But I don't feel threatened by that, for I have learned how, out of death, new life can be borne. I have learned that the life of the church encompasses so much more than a small handful of individuals. Life can carry on, even if it is not church life as we know it.

So it is that we have to constantly keep alert ... to watch for opportunity to make shifts and changes, always keeping the future goals in mind. We have to keep asking ourselves the key questions, which have more to do with enhancing the spiritual life of the community and its people ... and less to do with keeping the old forms of the institution going. That is when we come to realize that we don't have to give up the basic things of the church. But we do have to keep making adjustments. And we do have to learn to accept the adjustments when they are made.

Do you remember those old "dead" logs in the garden? It took a while, but when I was able to lay them in the earth and leave them for a while, new forms of life sprang forth because of their existence. Sometimes in the midst of our grief, we are called to give thanks for the life we have had ... and trust in the hope and the promise of better things for tomorrow.

One of the helpful things we can do when we hit difficult times in the life of a congregation is to remember the lives of the saints. Remember the stories of those who worked in the congregation. Remember, also, those people who have touched our individual lives in our own faith journey.

I do this kind of remembering with families at the time of a funeral. I ask them to tell me stories about why this individual was special to them. Often we start with the most recent memories - of sickness, of suffering, of approaching death. Then, cautiously, one person will chuckle as they say, "But that's not really what our mom was like," and then tell a story that describes Mom's spunk, or her wit, or her sensitivity. We all start to relax as the stories flow forth, tinged with a tear here ... and a burst of laughter there. Not only are individuals able to tell others what this person meant to them, but they are hearing different perspectives from each other ... and that is good.

So often, as these memories are shared, I have a profound sense that this life continues in its own way, and those involved feel more prepared to move toward whatever the future will hold.

Remember the saints: those who have built our churches, those who worked hard to see that the life of the congregation continues, even during the hard times. Think about their faith, their hope, the heritage that they preserved. Look beyond the despair of the moment, and discover the new ways by which the Spirit can direct us to leave a strong foundation for those who follow.

We need to think about these things. We need to talk about these things. We need to pray about these things. We need to give thanks for the church as we know it ... and feel assured that, in some way, it will be continued for our children, and their children.

Thanks be to God!

In The Bulb There Is A Flower

In the bulb there is a flower, in the seed, an apple tree,
in cocoons, a hidden promise: butterflies will soon be free!
In the cold and snow of winter there's a spring that waits to be,
unrevealed until its season, something God alone can see.

There's a song in every silence, seeking word and melody,
there's a dawn in every darkness, bringing hope to you and me.
From the past will come the future, what it holds, a mystery.
Unrevealed until its season, something God alone can see.

In our end is our beginning, in our time, infinity,
in our doubt there is believing, in our life, eternity.
In our death a resurrection; at the last, a victory,
unrevealed until its season, something God alone can see.

by Natalie Sleeth

Text: Natalie Sleeth
Text © *1986 Hope Publishing Co., Carol Stream, Il 60188.*
All rights reserved. Used by permission.

An Example Of Healing

I heard an example of healing the other day on a radio phone-in show. The topic dealt with men who refuse to pay child support.

One angry man lashed out at a woman, verbally, violently attacking her for what she had said. Then the very next caller, also a man, put things so quietly back into perspective by calling to say, "I don't agree with what the previous caller said ..." He then went on to make his own statement.

There was a healing touch in the way he handled the situation ... a simple righting of a wrong! All of us could do that if we wanted to.

The Generosity of One Man

Small communities can be harsh and judgmental. But often the thoughtfulness of one wise person can make all the difference.

It was the second fall after I was ordained. Because I had become exhausted, I found an excuse to head off to the city for a few days to try to break loose from the intricate concerns of a four-point Pastoral Charge.

As so often happens, I had barely left town when one of the elderly saints of the community died. She was someone I knew by name only.

The young Undertaker called me at my friend's home in the city, told me of the death, and suggested that the family wanted the funeral two days hence. That meant I had to get home almost immediately to prepare for a service. Those arrangements didn't suit me at all. His alternate suggestion was that he contact a neighboring minister to see if he could conduct the funeral on the suggested day... and those arrangements were confirmed back to me.

I got back to our little village the day after the funeral to find that all hell had broken loose. Certain people within the community were more than ready to run me out of town, "because you REFUSED to take Mrs. Brown's funeral!" There were accusations behind my back. There were thinly veiled insults to my face. There was definitely no generosity of spirit as the community heaped burning coals on my shoulders.

I was surprised, devastated, and totally helpless in defending myself. This was not a matter that could be explained away.

But one member of the Church Board went to bat for

me. He was the quietest of men. He seldom spoke out in meetings, and usually let his wife do the talking at home. That one man, after hearing more of those accusations, simply said, "Enough. I've heard enough of all this talk." He went on to recall what it is like to be young and inexperienced, and not always ready to make the best of judgment calls. He asked that people consider the whole circumstance. Had they considered the possibility that the Undertaker might have arranged things to fit his schedule ... My friend didn't cast aspersions in any one direction. He simply called people to be generous in their thinking, and in their talking. What was done was done!

Many times I think about the wisdom of that one man. I think about what a difference he made to my whole ministry, and my whole life. Because of the generosity of his spirit, and the way he stood beside me, he brought healing and health back into our midst.

Jesus and The Children

from The Family Story Bible. Illustrated by Margaret Kyle

Ralph Milton tells the following story, based on Matthew 19:13-15, Mark 10:13-16; and Luke 18:15-17.

Jesus liked children. And children liked Jesus.

Children liked Jesus because he smiled at them and laughed with them.

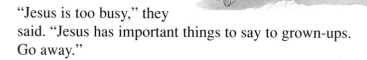

Sometimes the disciples tried to make the children go away.

"Jesus is too busy," they said. "Jesus has important things to say to grown-ups. Go away."

Jesus got upset when the disciples pushed the children away. "I want to be with the children," he said. "Please don't push them away."

"But why?" asked the disciples. "Grown ups are more important."

"No, they are not!" said Jesus. "Children are just as important. And grown-ups can learn many things from children."

"But grown-ups know more than children," the disciples

said.

"Grown-ups know many things," said Jesus. "But they don't understand some things. Some children understand love and trust better than grown-ups ..."

Jesus could see the grown-ups didn't know what he was talking about. So Jesus picked up a tiny child, a child just learning how to walk. The child snuggled up to Jesus, and tugged at his beard. Jesus laughed.

"Look at this child. This child doesn't know who I am. But the child can feel my love. And so the child trusts me. That's what God's Shalom is like."

Then Jesus gave the child a little hug and kiss. But some of the grown-ups still didn't understand.

Meeting The Moderator

As a single person, I have the best of both worlds. I enjoy children, and frequently invite them to spend time with me. They arrive clean, rested, enthused. We do many interesting things together. Then when they are tired, dirty, and a bit cranky, I drop them off at their own homes. ... The following is a story of a wonderful evening spent with special friends.

"Can we go over to your house now," the two kids begged, their eyes dancing with excitement. They hadn't met my visitor yet. They didn't know what it meat to be "Moderator of the United Church of Canada." They didn't even know if he liked kids or not ... But they trusted me when I asked them if they and their Great Grandmother, my friend and neighbour, would become my family for this evening, and would help me host my special guest.

The Right Reverend Stan McKay had spent the day visiting with representatives from the Peigan Nation and from our congregation. We toured strategic sites along the Old Man River. We talked about concerns having to do with the building of the Old Man River Dam. We talked about how the Native and Non-Native communities could benefit from working more closely with each other. We ate together, and we prayed together.

Now it was time for an evening of relaxation before tomorrow's church services and public gatherings.

Granny had put the roast in her oven, and added the potatoes and carrots and onions at just the right time. Obviously the kids had been shopping. Their new outfits were still starchy fresh. Ryan's clip-on tie was the first tie he had ever owned. One moment this 6-year old thought of himself as a young man. The next moment it was impossible for him to be anything but a kid.

"Can we go now," Dana begged. She could see it was going to take me a few minutes to talk with Granny and collect my steaming roaster full of goodies. Every hair was in place. I noticed she even had new barrettes for her braids. What a moment for a 5-year old.

"... Leave the inside door open," I shouted after the kids heading across the street. "I'll have my hands full with the hot food." But they were gone. Curiosity had won out over shyness.

I paused long enough for Granny to get her coat, and check that the oven was off. She was more reserved, but ever so proud. Before we reached the sidewalk, we could hear the laughter and the giggles. Not only had Ryan and Dana introduced themselves to Stan, but the three of them were on the living room floor playing ride-em cowboy.

Post Script

Sunday morning, as we came into the Pincher Creek Church Dana and Ryan were waiting to wave and catch our eye from the top step of the church. Their new clothes were rumpled from the previous evening's wear, but their faces shone and their hair was neatly brushed. They had a surprise of their own to share. When they went back to the farm that night, where they lived with their grandparents, they phoned their mom and told her about their exciting new friend.

"Mom," they shouted together. "He was wonderful. Couldn't you come to Church tomorrow? Couldn't you be there to meet him?" ... And she was there!

Miss Baxter Was Something Else!

Ralph Milton tells the following wonderful story on himself.

Every fall, when the bright-eyed children gather in church, I remember my first day of school. Like many children, I went singing into school, but soon had that singing silenced by a teacher who divided the class into "canaries and crows." I was one of the crows. It was years before I could sing again.

I was a desperately awkward teenager, but I had fantasies of becoming a great athlete. Those were shattered when I tried out for football. Trying to kick a field goal, I broke three fingers on the hand of the boy holding the ball. It was years before I would try any sport again.

But I also remember Miss Baxter who liked me, croaky voice, gangly legs and big nose. I hated that big nose. There was nothing uglier in the whole world than my big nose.

Miss Baxter liked me. She thought I could write. "Why not write an essay about noses?" she asked. "Go to the library and find out everything you can about noses." Lots of fine people had big noses, I discovered. I also discovered that it's more fun to laugh about things like noses, than it is to sulk about them.

Miss Baxter believed in my gifts. After a while, I began to believe in my gifts too. Every fall, when the bright-eyed children gather in church, I can believe in their gifts because Miss Baxter believed in mine.

Joseph and Jesus

Too often Joseph is treated like a bit-player in the Christmas Story.
The same thing has happened to a lot of the men in today's society.
Why? What are we prepared to do about that attitude?

In the Christmas story, the person who is given least
attention, less even than the sheep, is Joseph. But time
and again my heart goes out to this man. Right from the
beginning, it is impossible to imagine how hard it must
have been for Joseph. Barely is he engaged, when his
bride-to-be disappears for three months without saying a
word to anyone. Then, when she returns, it is obvious
by her appearance and by what she says, that she is pregnant. Joseph lashes out at her in anger and despair, only
to have some kind of dream in which he is told this child
has been fathered by God. Now he, Joseph, has been
asked to assume the role of surrogate parent.

Whatever it was that went through Joseph's mind in
the succeeding six months, when we think of him at the
time of Mary's delivery, we find a man who appears to
be more than attentive to her needs. He stands by her
while others scoff at her unfaithfulness. He does what
he can to make the journey to Bethlehem bearable.
Later, he flees with her and the child to Egypt when they
learn of Herod's jealous plot to kill all the newborns in
his kingdom.

We aren't sure how old Jesus was when Joseph died.
I have always understood that Joseph raised the lad, and
apprenticed him in his own trade. But our suspicion is
that, as the eldest child, Jesus had to assume family
responsibilities for his brothers and sisters while he was
still quite young. For the sake of argument, let's assume
Jesus might have been fifteen years of age when Joseph

died. Those fifteen years would give time for some kind of father-son bond to develop. But think of the hazards along the way!

What kind of relationship did Joseph and Jesus have? It is hard for two men in the same house to form any kind of bond. Their home would be typical in that Mary would do a lot of the nurturing, though probably Joseph would take Jesus to synagogue to sit with the men. What about their time together? Were there the silences that so often permeated father-son relationships? Where there times when the lad was left to wonder, "Does he like me?" Did Jesus ever ask, "Why doesn't he try to understand me?" Was the relationship made even tougher because these two may not have been, as they say, "related by blood." How did the power-struggle go? What happened once they started working together? Or were things better defined then, with one the apprentice, and the other the master?

My heart goes out to Joseph. I know how distanced an adopted child can feel in even the kindest of family situations. I know how impossible it is to assume certain footholds that others take for granted. Joseph was a surrogate father in a situation not of his own choosing.

My suspicion is that Jesus probably had as temperamental a youth as do a lot of young boys. This is why, by the time he reached his twenties he had to get completely away from home, and from family expectations, to search out who he really was.

The wonderful thing is that, when Jesus emerged from his searching after himself, he emerged with a whole new vision of how people should live in relationship with each other, and with God. In a healthy, respectful way, he explained to the people that God was like a Father. And as he drew others, especially young men, to work with him - the terms of their relationship had to do with mutual respect, and with sharing even their deepest feelings. It was what we might call, today, "healthy male bonding."

As a woman, I can only stand on the outside and look in. But I would love to overhear a group of men talk about Joseph and Jesus. I would love to hear them discuss whether or not Jesus' relationship with Joseph prepared him for this. This wasn't the norm in a Jewish home of the day.

But Jesus' teachings bear witness to his experience. He had a way with people, with getting them to think of God in intimate terms. These reflections would suggest that, as a lad, he and Joseph shared at a much deeper level than just a few grunts and a lot of silences.

As we hear Jesus talking heart-to-heart with his closest friends, I sense that ability to talk so personally didn't just happen over night. Jesus didn't feel the need to act in an authoritarian way. Nor did he hide behind a mystique when relating with others. He had learned at Joseph's knee how to talk with another about the lessons learned from life. And he and Joseph respected each other in the process.

Much, much later, as we watch Jesus teach Peter the virtues of patience, again I see the mirror image of mentor and apprentice in the carpenter shop. I see Joseph allowing the lad, Jesus, to make his mistakes. I see Joseph reminding the lad that no one is perfect ... that one must often carry on in spite of mistakes made in the past.

Listen to the Christmas story with new ears. Imagine yourself in Joseph's shoes, raising a son whose parentage was uncertain. Imagine Joseph giving that son the gift of a grounding so solid that the lad would dare to teach others a whole new way of thinking about relationships: with each other, and with God.

One writer on the subject of the relationship of fathers and sons says that for a man to be truly himself, he must be born three times. The first time, he is born out of the womb of his mother. The second time, he is born again out of his relationship with his father, another man like himself. Then he is born the third time out of his own self - when he comes to that point in life where he takes hold and says "I am responsible for my own life. I assume that responsibility!" (Guy Corneau in Absent Fathers, Lost Sons)

Joseph, in this light, becomes the hero of the Jesus-story. So much of his character is evident even before the lad is born. Notice the way Joseph stays with Mary through all those months, even though this conception is not of his doing. Notice the tender way in which he cares for her in the terribly difficult times that mark the later stages of her pregnancy. Notice the relationship that he developed with the lad who is later to be called "Messiah," "Son of God!" Notice the way he taught the lad the importance of being able to show softness, of risking himself by sharing his feelings.

Think about Joseph's tremendous capacity to love ... and be thankful!

Getting To The Front Of The Stable

Who put Joseph in the back of the stable?
Who dressed him in brown, put a staff in his hand,
   and told him to stand in the back of the creche,
   background for the magnificent light of the Madonna?

God-chosen, this man Joseph was faithful
   in spite of the gossip in Nazareth,

in spite of the danger from Herod.
This man, Joseph, listened to angels
and it was he who named the Child Emmanuel.

Is this a man to be stuck for centuries
in the back of the stable?
Actually, Joseph probably stood in the doorway
guarding the mother and child
or greeting shepherds and kings.

When he wasn't in the doorway,
he was probably urging Mary to get some rest,
gently covering her with his cloak,
assuring her that he would watch the Child.
Actually, he probably picked the Child up in his arms
and walked him in the night,
patting him lovingly
until he closed his eyes.

This Christmas, let us give thanks to God
for this man of incredible faith
into whose care God placed the Christ Child.
As a gesture of gratitude,
let's put Joseph in the front of the stable
where he can guard and greet
and cast an occasional glance
at this Child who brought us life.

Ann Weems

Wise Words

A wife may fuss and fume because the men don't immediately come when the dinner call goes out. "But I realize now," one woman told me, speaking of her husband and his dad, long after the latter had died, "that a lot of problems were being talked out, and a lot of learning was taking place..."

GOD bless
Our home

LOVE
PEACE

DON BRESTLER '95

Cowboy Christmas Gathering

We have held other Cowboy Christmas Services, and
felt the community was most appreciative. But the ser-

vice this year was most touching of all.

The formula was the same. An *ad hoc* planning group gathered in early November to share their ideas. Don Brestler talked about design possibilities for a bulletin cover. Jackie Therrieult had been thinking about what the special music might be. We named congregational sing-along pieces. We talked about bringing a saddle, some pack-trip gear, and a barb wire Christmas wreath to lend atmosphere at the front of the Sanctuary.

But always we drew each other back to our central commitment. We didn't have a Cowboy Service because it was gimmicky, nor cute. And we didn't intend that it be a performance. This was about gathering folk together to acknowledge a style of living and believing that was special. Each year the invitation to the community included the following:

"Many who don't regularly attend Sunday Worship still have deep spiritual roots. Our 'Christmas Gathering' gives opportunity to share these values in the context of a worship service."

I'm not sure why the Gathering took on the deeper dimension this year. But I know that at one point or another, every eye blinked a tear or two. Memories of times past came to mind, of going to school on the old horse, of a favorite place where children go to dream, of sharing with a dear old friend across a lonely prairie. Memories came, too, of the special ones whose funeral we had attended in recent years; and of others who continue to wage their silent battles with cancer, and heart conditions, and the like. The lump in the throat, the touch of an understanding arm from the person beside you, the prayer for a proud heritage that we can pass on to our children ... these were all part of our being together. We bowed our heads in gratitude, and gave thanks.

Afterwards, over steaming bowls of baked beans and home made bread and cups of cowboy coffee, old friends met to exchange greetings, recall stories, and enjoy a good laugh together. We sang "Happy trails to you till we meet again," and felt blessed by God as we took our leave.

A Story About John Ware

Told to children of all ages at one Cowboy Christmas Service
written by Bronze Sculptor Leon Levesque of Pincher Creek, Alberta

John Ware, the famous cowboy, was born in slavery in the southern United States, but spent much of his life in Alberta and became one of our best loved and respected ranchers.

Little is known of his early life. His father was a free slave, but his mother was owned by a Mr. Chauncey of Southern Carolina. They had ten children. When the Civil War ended the slaves found themselves free and with a power and responsibility they did not know how to use.

The story of John Ware's coming to Alberta in 1882 starts with one of Tom Lynch's cattle drives from Idaho. Bill Moody and his friend, John Ware, were hired on as drovers. Negroes weren't supposed to be good cowboys, so John was given an old saddle and a gentle horse and made to ride "drag," the worst job, at the end of the herd, where the dust, flies and "meadow muffins" are the thickest. A few days later John asked Lynch if he could maybe have a "betta saddle and a waus hoss." Now nothing excites a bunch of cowboys more than putting a greenhorn on a horse that will buck, especially a black man who asked for it. They had a notorious bucking horse in the remuda. The cowboys gathered around to see the fun and watch this newcomer bite the dust. The saddling done, John climbed aboard, dug in his spurs, slapped the horse with his hat and gave him his head. To the amazement of all, he rode like an expert cowboy - which he was. And he won the admiration and respect of everyone ...

After reaching their destination, across the Highwood River west of Calgary, in September of 1882, John Ware was persuaded by Fred Stinson, the manager of the Bar U Ranch, to stay and work with him ...

Later, he acquired his own land and livestock. Many stories were related about John Ware, telling about his skills of riding horses and handling cattle, his phenomenal strength and kind heart. It seems that everybody who knew him had only good things to say about the gentle giant, a pioneer of the Alberta plains.

The Place Where I Worship

Lyric by Florence Starr and Ray Foster

Oh the place where I worship is the wide open spaces,
Built by the Hand of the Lord!
Where the trees of the forest are like pipes of an organ
and the breeze plays an Amen chord.
Oh the stars are the candles and they light up the mountains,
Mountains are altars of God.
Oh the place where I worship is the wide open spaces,
Where the sun warms the peaceful sod.

There's a carpet of green and a skyblue roof above;

I'm welcome there alone, or with the one I love.
In your heart take a good look,
If you follow the good book, you're sure to find your reward.
Oh the place where I worship is the wide open spaces,
Built by the Hand of the Lord.

(Recitation lines)
The place where I worship is the wide open spaces
Yes, built by the Hand of the Lord!
And He has given it to you and me
For all the world to see.
There are no doors, no bars - And all are free!
There in the air, like a joyous prayer,
You can hear Him say: "This is your country, this is your home;
Keep its splendor, and guard its glory!"

It's a song of freedom coming from
The valley to the hilltops - It never, never stops!
And all the birds on the wing are like a choir.
You can hear them sing: "You're free to worship here -
All creeds, all races are one before God ..."
As you rest beside a silver stream
There pours into your soul
A feeling of peace and quiet
And You give thanks to Him
For making the eye of your heart see
The heritage He has given - to you and to me.

Beethoven Helps Us Celebrate Easter

*Beethoven's masterpiece of music was the "Ode To Joy" It is the
final movement of the eloquent, passionate Ninth Symphony. At this
moment in the musical work, the singers can keep silent no longer.
With their voices, they announce a powerful expression of worship.*

Would you believe that the music for the "Ode To
Joy" was written by a totally deaf person? Would you
believe, also, that it was written at a time in history when
it seemed the world order was about to totally collapse?

Just at the point when Napoleon believed himself to
be invincible, there was insurrection and revolt among
his soldiers. Just when he had humiliated Austria by
forcing her to surrender three million inhabitants in a so-
called "Peace Treaty" (Treaty of Pressbury, 1805), trade
blockades in Europe and turbulence in the Americas set
the groundwork for the French Revolution. Napoleon
bled Poland and Czechoslovakia of billion of dollars so
he could maintain his armies of occupation ... and the
mood of the land seethed with ferment, hatred, and
despair.

This was the mood of the land at the time when
Beethoven, Hayden, and Mozart wrote their music. All
of them lived in Vienna as contemporaries!

Add to this the additional growing burden that
Beethoven had to bear. He, a pianist and composer,
slowly became totally deaf. Think of the months of dis-
tress and misery he endured when even the loudest of
talking and the loudest of music was taken from him.
Ever since he was four years old, music had been his
life. It gave him escape from a drunkard father. It was a
solace when, as a teenager, he lost his mother. It was a
means of support when he assumed responsibility for his

two younger brothers and a sister.

We can only imagine the times Ludwig despaired as he saw his world crumble. But he swore that fate would never drag him down. One of his biographers wrote, "With Beethoven for an opponent, fate hardly had a chance!" He never lost faith in himself. What is more, as the "Ode to Joy" attests, he never lost trust in God!

Out of the darkness, the whole of the Ninth symphony, and especially the "Ode to Joy," speaks to us of raw faith and tremendous courage. It is a very human, very personal story-melody that moves hearts, that inspires confidence, and ignites candles of hope.

This kind of music leaves us standing on tiptoes, and that is what the Easter Experience is all about. We come to this place of sanctuary from our everyday lives hungry, needing to be fed. Each of us carry our own silent burdens of pain, of grief, of despair. Now, for these few moments, we are invited to lay our burdens aside. We are invited to put on our finest, and share of our best. We are invited, through song and prayer, ... to join in the celebration, ... to acknowledge the promise, ... to think about what is good. We look around us and see familiar faces, and remember their stories as we pray for the sorrows others have faced.

Beethoven's music ... the Scriptural story ... and our own experience help us as we try to span the gap between reality and ecstasy ... between the surface world ... and the ultimate realm of meaning that God has promised.

Joyful, Joyful

Joyful, joyful we adore thee, God of glory, Lord of love;
hearts unfold like flowers before thee, opening to the sun above.
Melt the clouds of sin and sadness, drive the dark of doubt away;
giver of immortal gladness, fill us with the light of day.

All thy works with joy surround thee, earth and heaven reflect thy rays;
stars and angels sing around thee, centre of unbroken praise.
Field and forest, vale and mountain, flowery meadow, flashing sea,
chanting bird and flowing fountain, sound their praise eternally.

You are giving and forgiving, ever blessing, ever blest,
well-spring of the joy of living, ocean depth of happy rest!
Source of grace and fount of blessing, let your light upon us shine;
teach us how to love each other, lift us to the joy divine.

Mortals join the mighty chorus, which the morning stars began;
God's own love is reigning o'er us, joining people hand in hand.
Ever singing, march we onward, victors in the midst of strife;
joyful music leads us sunward in the triumph song of life.
(words written by Henry van Dyke, melody is "Ode to Joy"
written by Beethoven)

Congregational Prayer

Let us remember the long journey we have traveled
through this past year.
Let us think about the many storms we have faced.
Let us think about the way we have been caught up in tur-
moil on behalf of others close to us.
Let us think about how we have been disturbed because of
things that have happened in the communities of which we
are a part.

*There is so much that has been painful ... so much that
raised responses of fear ... So much that
has caused stress, and has drained us physically and emo-
tionally.*

*Let us look back, again, and think about some of the words
of understanding, the gestures ... the indicators of hope ...
that helped us carry on.*
*Let us remember the tiny gifts of life we were able to share
with another ... to help make their burden a little easier.
So often we have found it to be true that when we give, that
is when we receive a certain sense of
satisfaction ... and joy ... and strength for ourselves.*

*As we celebrate our Easter Faith, O God, help us rise
above the ordinary. Help us overlook, for a moment, the
turbulence. Help us find strength in believing. Help us
find joy in celebrating. Amen*

Postlude

I'll never forget the little canary that we brought into
the sanctuary last week to help us celebrate Easter
Sunday.

At first, I think she felt pretty insignificant in this big
sanctuary ... timid and afraid as people gathered.
Through the first half of the service, she seemed ready to
take off, if given a chance. Then, when she heard the
sound of the piano and the organ during the offertory,
something touched her heart. The fear subsided ... and
she discovered that, in her own tiny way, she too could
contribute to our Easter celebrations.

From then on, she sang so beautifully ... so powerfully ... as I spoke, as we prayed, but particularly as the choirs sang their "Ode To Joy!"

What more fitting parable could we find ... for us, and for our church community. We each have something unique and special to give. And as we give, the best gift of all is the joy and satisfaction that comes with finding ways to share with each other.

Thanks be to God.   Amen!

Feelings of Belonging

"Amid misfortune, there is fortune."
old Korean Proverb

Brad was nine years old when the accident happened. It was the Christmas holidays and he, along with a number of other boys, was playing in the skating rink - climbing where they shouldn't have been climbing. One minute, he was holding tight on an overhanging beam. The next minute he was lying in an unconscious heap on the ice, eight feet below. X-rays showed he had a four inch crack in his skull ... For the next several days no one could be certain if there was more major damage.

We can hardly begin to imagine the turmoil, and fear, and upset of that young family during the following weeks. True, their first concern was for Brad, in an Intensive Care Unit in a hospital two hours' drive from home. But there were the three younger children, too. And what about the costs - since they had forgotten to mail in this year's Blue Cross Coverage? Nor could the parents live in the Intensive Care Unit with their son.

I tell this true story because any of us can imagine

ourselves having some part in the story: being in the place of those young parents; or offering to take the kids and the dog; or starting to collect some money; or phoning city relatives to find a place for the parents to stay; or dashing in to be with the family, since their own parents lived too far away.

I tell this story because some of you know what it is like: the endlessly long hours in that ICU; the helplessness of a community that could only hold its breath and pray for good news; the love and support of people who suddenly realize how much this family, complete outsiders only a few years previous, had come to be an important part of the community.

Later, Brad came home ... and began moaning because he had to wait a whole year before he could go to hockey school. Later, when the bills had been paid, and the neck brace and support were returned, life returned to a more normal routine ... in the family ... and in the community. But it was never quite the same again. Something special had bonded us together in a way that was unique and wonderful.

Brad's dad put it best by recalling how it was when he first arrived in the community. He was your typical hippie of the late Sixties. He moved in to a very small, very conservative rural community that wasn't used to hippies! But during those hours in the Intensive Care Unit, while he wondered and waited, a lot of things came into focus for that young father. The community showed him that he and his family were an important part of their town. After so many years, the community saw this to be an opportunity to reach out and embrace and claim the family.

Brad's dad told how these events caused him to change his mind. Until then, he had been thinking about pulling up stakes to move elsewhere, again. Now all that had changed. He had changed. He had an identity. He belonged to the community. He had roots. He had responsibility. Maybe there would be times when he could help others as he had been helped.

The whole circumstance surrounding the accident became a kind of mountain top experience for many of us. It lifted us above the everyday, mundane, careless routine of life ... and showed us how special we could be to each other when the crunch comes! It changed lives, deepened commitments, made us feel like we were privileged to be able to accept responsibility for each other ... We knew that we wanted to be committed to each other.

Lovely To Look At

Ministers can get pretty cynical about weddings. Too many are more about show than substance. But there was one I will never forget.

Mike and Jean and Mike's two girls had been living together for the last two years. While they were building strong relationships among themselves, they were also fighting for custody rights for the girls. Mike's "Ex" wasn't making the job easy. She didn't really want the responsibility that goes with mothering a seven and a nine year old. But she certainly didn't want him to have the satisfaction of having clear custody either.

The couple had known for some time that they wanted to get married - in front of family and friends. But such arrangements aren't easy when two people are working shift work in Fort McMurray, raising a family, meeting a seemingly endless number of court dates ... and with the rest of the family living hundreds of miles south, in a small village near the American Border.

My first interview with them was when they came home at Christmas. The second meeting would be two days before the actual service. The radiant glow on their faces at that second interview spoke louder than their words. The court had cleared the custody question, and we would be truly marrying a ready-made family.

Those last few minutes before a wedding have their own momentum for a minister. Guests coming, organist playing, nervous groom, elegant bride trying to outwit the prairie wind as she makes her way from the car to the church ...

This time, there was more! The girls were simply beautiful. Just for that moment they stole the show. Their hairdos ... their lovely dresses ... their glowing faces told so much about how important this occasion was for them. They came in with the bride, but I had to ask, "Has your dad seen you all dressed up?" Before that traditional moment when the groom sees his bride coming down the aisle, he and his daughters had to have their own moment. "He has just got to see how lovely you two really are ... We'll get on with the wedding in a couple of minutes." I had them follow me down to the basement, where their father was waiting.

Tears welled out of his eyes and mine as he followed me into the sanctuary that afternoon. Never did a family wedding seem more right, nor the processional hymn more appropriate:

> *"Now thank we all our God*
> *with heart, and hands, and voices*
> *Who wondrous things hath done,*
> *in whom His world rejoices ..."*

Blackfoot Prayer
Napi Friendship Centre Cross-Cultural Days' Blessing

Members from the communities of Pincher Creek. Alberta, and the Peigan Nation share an annual cross-cultural celebration. The Blessing Ceremony opens the conference. Its main purpose is to receive blessings from the Creator for the successful delivery of the conference. An Elder is called on to lead a prayer in his own words. The following is in interpretation of one such prayer.

Oh Creator, giver of life, I humble myself for you to
     assist me today.
I am preparing my pipe to call on you today
     to help us in our efforts to achieve understanding
     of people here with us tonight.

The sweetgrass smudge I have in front of me brings
     you the message from all of us here,
and all of the spirits of those who have gone before us.
     I ask that you accept and be here with us.
     I am preparing my mind, body, and spirit with this
smudge,
so I come to you pure and from my heart.
The words I am about to bring you represent all the
     people here
          that I am about to share my pipe with.

Oh Creator, I ask that you look upon us and guide us
     through our journey,
     not only tonight, but every day.
          Oh Father Sun please continue to shine on us
               and provide us with your powerful nourishment.
          Oh Mother Earth we are very grateful
for your medicines, food, and shelter ...

Together we must all strive to give this group of people
our support, prayers, knowledge, and wisdom
to achieve better understanding.

Oh Creator we will do our best to respect the land
and all that goes with it.
Oh Creator we will preserve it for our grandchildren.

Oh Creator, the effort of these people needs your
direction.
Please support them.
Make the next four days and nights successful for them.

I will now share my pipe...
(interpretation of prayer prepared by Quinton Crow Shoe)

The Pipe Ceremony

The main purpose of the Pipe Ceremony is to sanction
the Conference officially. It begins with the burning of
sweetgrass. The keeper of the pipe holds his hands over
the sweetgrass smoke and passes them over his head,
preparing his mind for prayer. He then cups the smoke
and passes it over his heart, since it is from the heart that
the prayer is uttered. When this is finished, the stone
bowl and wooden stem of the pipe are joined together,
making the pipe complete.

Now it is filled with tobacco, a sacred gift from the
spirit world. It is then passed over the sweetgrass smoke,
stem first and then bowl. The pipe is rotated over the
smoke in the same direction as the sun's rotation. This
makes the pipe spiritually alive, sacred and powerful.
The pipe is lit and then lifted, stem upward, toward the

Creator, because He is above all things and comes first before all things. A prayer of thanks is directed to the Creator for his love and kindness in giving life to all things. Thanks is given also for the pipe as an instrument of prayer, a channel of blessing, and the medium for spiritual intervention.

When the prayer is done the pipe is lowered, stem pointing down, and thanks given for all things growing on earth. It is then pointed in four directions, to call upon the powers of those directions. The pipe is then passed to the person on the left, who takes the pipe by the stem and smokes a few puffs, signaling his or her participating in the conference. He also publicly states his reasons for supporting the event. Each person in turn takes the pipe and smokes a few puffs, thinking of the Creator above and the earth below, and the four directions around him. The ceremony brings him into contact and harmony with all these things. The four directions signify the four life-giving elements: sun, earth, water and air, as well as the four directions, the four seasons and the four phases in a person's life.

After the pipe has concluded its circuit, it is then returned to the holder, who offers another prayer. The pipe and bowl are separated and laid down, indicating closure to the ceremony.

(notes prepared by Shirley Crowshoe)

Saskatoon Berries

The Saskatoon berries served up at the Opening of the Cross Cultural Conference are considered one of the most important foods used by the Piikani (Peigan) people. Not only are they nutritious in themselves, they are also symbols of all plant life, and the nutrients they provide. The berries are prepared as a soup-like dish and served first to lead the ceremonies.

Protocol has everyone in attendance take one berry from the serving and pray in their own way, as a way of contributing to the support of the gathering. This single "prayer" berry is collected and returned to the earth by a delegated individual, as a way to ensure the continuing fertility of the earth.

Everyone can then enjoy their bowl of Saskatoon berries! Kianniayi!

(notes prepared by Shirley Crowshoe)

Looking Back On A Full Life
Paraphrase of Psalm 23

The last words I remember Grandma Sasse asking us to say with her were the words of the Twenty-Third Psalm. She had lived a long and full life. I'm sure she would have appreciated the following.

God has walked with me; I could ask nothing more.
God has given me green meadows to laugh in,
clear streams to think beside, untrodden paths to explore.

When I thought the world rested on my shoulders,
God put things into perspective,
When I lashed out at an unfair world, God calmed me down.
When I drifted into harmful ways, God straightened me out.
God was with me all the way.

I do not know what lies ahead, but I am not afraid.
I know you will be with me.
Even in death, I will not despair.

You will comfort and support me.
Though my eye dims and my mind dulls,
you will continue to care about me.
Your touch will soothe the tensions in my temples;
my fears will fade away.
I am content.

In life, in death, in life beyond death, God is with me.
All through life, I have found goodness in people.
When life ends, I expect to be gathered
into the ultimate goodness of God.

by James Taylor

On The Edge Of The Holy

*Each year, just before Lent begins, we read an account of the
Transfiguration story. It is a story in which the disciples, who were
with Jesus, had a particular awareness of the presence of God.
Literally, this was a mountain top experience! (Luke 9:28-36)*

One Sunday, at our youth service, a visitor by the
name of Angeline sang "Jesus Loves Me." Her voice
was so clear, and the arrangement was so beautiful, all of
us were moved. Many felt they should clap for her, yet
no one wanted to be the first to intrude on the moment.
Afterwards, I overheard someone express the same thing
I felt. They said, "It was too beautiful. I just couldn't
clap!"

It seemed appropriate for that experience to happen
just as we were about to read the Transfiguration story.
Both this story, and the Biblical story, helps us think

about the awesome experiences that have happened in each of our lives. Both these stories invite us to bring to mind other occasions when we have been touched, deep inside, by some experience that made a difference to the rest of our life.

I think of the day my friend Marlene talked with me about her open-heart surgery ... and what an impact that had on her life. She started by telling me about her condition, and how the possibility of surgery hung over her for years. Finally she had the operation, and a new vitality filled her body because her malfunctioning heart finally worked as it was meant to work.

"But the thing that really moved me," Marlene said, "was when I thought about the fact my heart actually stopped for those moments when they did the repair! It actually stopped! The adjustments were made, and then it started to work again, in the proper way!"

That awareness has made Marlene marvel at and value the gift of life in a way few of us can appreciate. That awareness, and the awesomeness of that experience, had made Marlene treasure each moment ... and look for ways she could share those moments as her gift of gratitude!

My own memory of seeing beyond the veil of the ordinary happened one day as I made a climb in the Canadian Rockies from Cameron Lake over the Carthew Summit and back toward the Waterton Townsite. Being a person who finds it hard to stick to an ordinary trail, my hiking partner and I decided to follow through on an extra challenge, and climb to the crest of one of the ridges, in search of mountain goats! Only after we started, did we realize the danger of clinging on the thin layer of shale that covered an otherwise sheer rock face. There was nothing to cling to. The shale kept moving

under us. It moved down an eighty degree slope with
nothing to stop it for hundreds of feet. To stay still, we
had to keep moving. To make progress toward the ridge
(and the only safe way of escape), we had to move faster
than the sliding shale ... and never stop, no matter how
tired we got! To make a long story short, we eventually
got to the top. There we found an even more sheer, ver-
tical face on the opposite side. It was a place of awesome beauty, and of true terror. Eventually we worked
our way along the crest of that ridge, and back to safety.

Afterwards, I wondered why I hadn't taken pictures of
the scenes from the ridge. Then I realized I didn't
because I couldn't. Just like I couldn't clap for
Angeline. I knew that something very special had happened to me that day. I couldn't snap the camera
because what happened was too profound an experience.
In that climb I had come face-to-face with death. That
was when I realized just how much I valued life. I was
able to keep moving and not give up because I had to
keep moving. Life was too precious. Ahead were
important things God expected me to do!

That experience gave my life new purpose, new
momentum. I discovered each moment to be a treasure
beyond worth!

It is with this understanding that we look again at our
Gospel story, told to us by each of the Disciples. A few
of them were there with Jesus when something unique
and awesome happened. They had no words to explain
how or what ... But they knew that they saw their friend
Jesus standing alongside two of the great holy men of
old, alongside Moses and Elijah. They knew that they
stood there, together, on the edge of the holy. And they
realized that the Great God Almighty was better known
by them because of that experience.

Death Comes As A Friend

I am acutely aware, at the time of death, that the funeral service is for the living. It is important that family members share their memories and stories with each other. It is important that the hymns and scripture lessons give expression to the things they believe. In Mrs. Allan's case, this was complicated because her daughter, at 77 years of age, felt very alone, and had forgotten how it was when her mother was young.

When you are almost a hundred years old and have been confined to bed in a nursing home for more than a decade, death can be a friend. Anne knew that her mother passionately wanted to "go to her reward" long before she went. Anne knew, too, that her sisters and the other members of the family already acted as if mother was gone. The old lady's house had been sold, her belongings distributed, power of attorney given over ... Faithfully, Anne made the trip to our community twice a year, in spite of the distance, in spite of her own health, in spite of the fact she really had no place to stay when she got here ... She faithfully endeavored to maintain the weak spark of communication with the frail body that lay helpless for so long.

So many things couldn't be said. So many things would never be said. The frustration and the anger slowly churned in the depths of Anne's being. But, like her mother had shown her, she remained gentle, gracious, and loyal to the end.

When the end did come, the first thing Anne felt was relief - for herself, and for her mother. The next thing she felt was empty, drained, and so very alone. When she got to my office, she had little to say except "so be it."

I asked her to tell me about her mother ... But there

wasn't that much to tell from this past decade ... So unfair ... so wanting to die ... She could only say, "Death has come as a friend!"

When I asked her to think back to the rest of her mother's life, it seemed so distant ... for Anne was, herself, a great grandmother now. "Let me see ... I haven't thought about those things for so long ... They don't really seem to be that important ..." I could understand her difficulty, but I was not content to leave her there.

From others in our town, I got a few stories about when the family had their business on Main Street, and when those three daughters charmed the teenage boys, and when families went on Sunday picnics together. Stories were told of this woman's skills as a hairdresser and dressmaker. Word pictures were painted describing her garden. Accolades were given telling of her volunteer work with the Hospital.

From the history books, I noted that she was born the same year the whole of the British Empire celebrated Queen Victoria's Diamond Jubilee ... And she was four years old when that beloved Monarch died, after a reign of 64 years. Here, also, was a woman who was 21 years old at the time of 'The Great Flu Epidemic.' "So it is not surprising," I said in my funeral tribute, "that a person of her nature and loyalty to the crown would quickly sign up as a volunteer to do hospital work in the city, where she could help care for patients and staff ... nor is it surprising that she enjoyed the sisterhood of membership in the Imperial Order of The Daughters of the Empire."

I recalled snippets of her life as others in the community had remembered her ... so we could look beyond the endless hours she lay in bed, her alert mind caught in a tired body.

I drew a parallel between her life and the story of Tabitha (Dorcas) in Acts 9:36, 37. Tabitha gathered so many of the needy women of her community around her. She taught them to sew, so they could make a living for themselves. She gave them a sisterhood to which they could belong, so they didn't feel totally abandoned. She helped them regain their sense of self-worth by talking to them about a God who loved them, and a Saviour who expressed God's compassion in human ways ... I reminded everyone that it is through the stories of women like that that all of our lives are enriched.

We concluded with a prayer that the Jews recite annually on The Day of Atonement. It is "In Memory of Mother."

"I remember thee in this solemn hour, my dear mother. I remember the days when thou didst dwell on earth, and thy tender love watched over me like a guardian angel. Thou hast gone from me, but the bond which unites our souls can never be severed; thine image lives within my heart. May the merciful Father reward thee for the faithfulness and kindness thou hast shown me; may he lift up the light of his countenance upon thee, and grant thee eternal peace. Amen."

Ministers do many things for others. Just one letter of appreciation, such as I received from this grateful daughter, makes all the work worthwhile. I believe I gifted her with a fresh and dear memory of her mother. She, in turn, gifted me with the sincerity of her gratitude.

Dear Joyce,

I have been sitting here, glancing back and forth from my writing paper to the last blooming flowers in my garden, wondering how to find words to thank you for mother's funeral service. Never before have I heard a service where the minister has so obviously done her homework, using many sources of information, tying it all to historical facts, and even dressing in plaid for a dear Scottish lady. I'll never forget it - nor you.

I came home wishing I had had the chance to be a member of your congregation. I know that if I had, you would have been not only my spiritual mentor, but also my friend.

Concluding Prayer

In the privacy of your heart, pause to think back over your own life journey.

Imagine yourself turning the pages of the photo album of your life.

Search out the places and occasions that have been special to you ...

and for these, give thanks ...

Look for those reminders, half forgotten, half submerged, of the people whose lives have touched yours ....

people who have helped you in your pilgrimage.

And for these people, give thanks!

Don't deny the painful memories.

Let them come back to you.

Look back on them from a new perspective.

Think about how they touched you ... changed you ...

maybe even how they caused you to grow in understanding and wisdom.

Remember that these, too, have been God-given moments.

Forgive yourself for the mistakes you have made ...

and allow the healing love of God to help you carry on.

As you move from one page of your album to another,

appreciate the uniqueness and sacredness of your journey.
Notice those times when the companionship of others
has made things easier.
Notice, too, those occasions when a strength beyond
your own strength
has carried you through.

Finally, pause but a moment to anticipate the pictures
that will tell your stories of today ... and tomorrow ...
Have you made laughter a regular part of life?
Have you been able to rise above your grief and pain
by reaching beyond your doubts?
Have you been able to find nourishment for your soul?

Lord, teach us to pray. We ask this in your name.
Amen